Teaching Conflict Resolution
with the
Rainbow Kids Program

Barbara Porro

Illustrated by Peaco Todd

Association for Supervision and Curriculum Development
Alexandria, Virginia USA

Association for Supervision and Curriculum Development
1703 N. Beauregard St. · Alexandria, VA 22311-1714 USA
Telephone: 800-933-2723 or 703-578-9600 · Fax: 703-575-5400
Web site: http://www.ascd.org · E-mail: member@ascd.org

ASCD publications present a variety of viewpoints. The views expressed or implied in this book should not be interpreted as official positions of the Association.

Illustrated by Peaco Todd.
Printed in the United States of America.

ASCD Product No. 101247
ASCD member price: $20.95   nonmember price: $24.95

s4/2002

Library of Congress Cataloging-in-Publication Data

Porro, Barbara.
  Teaching conflict resolution with the Rainbow Kids Program / Barbara Porro ; illustrated by Peaco Todd.
      p. cm.
Includes bibliographical references and index.
  ISBN 0-87120-598-X (alk. paper)
  1. Conflict management--Study and teaching (Primary) 2. Behavior modification. 3. Classroom management. I. Title.
  LB3011.5 .P67 2002
  372.13'93--dc21
                                        2001008539

Teaching Conflict Resolution
with the Rainbow Kids Program

Acknowledgments

My heartfelt thanks to kind friends and colleagues whose generous support and encouragement made this book possible:

Sue Kimber, editor par excellence, for smoothing out the rough edges on early and late drafts and for masterfully reorganizing the text; Diane Hart, for cheering me on from beginning to end, for overhauling the look and feel of the manuscript, and for suggesting I call ASCD; Emma Bragdon, gentle teacher, for offering feedback from her enlightened perspective and shedding light on my blind spots; Peaco Todd, collaborator and artist, for enlivening these ideas with her capricious cartoons; Holly Melton, spinner of children's tales, for adding flow and sparkle to *The Rainbow Kids Story*; master teacher Julie Johnson, for steadfastly e-mailing her evaluative feedback and brilliant ideas, fresh from her sunny classroom where magic happens on a daily basis; Anabel Jensen, for her encouragement and expertise about emotional learning; Lois Byrd, for reminding me of my worth and helping me get what I deserve; Pat Korb, for kicking off my personal journey down the path of self-awareness; Craig Baker, for generously giving me time, space, and freedom to write this book; Annie Niehaus, soul sister and confidant, for believing in me and lighting my way to wholeness; and my daughter Audrey, for inspiring me daily with her gift of pure love.

For their thoughtful comments on various drafts of the manuscript and for their enthusiasm for the *Rainbow Kids Program* and for me personally, I thank Marie Crawford, Catherine Crawford, Larissa Keet, Marilyn Ferris, Kay Sandburg, Julie Propp, Jeanne Holmes, Susan Beekman, and John Swanson.

Heartfelt thanks to the Rainbow Kid teachers of San Mateo County who tested and refined these ideas and contributed dazzling ideas of their own.

Part 1

All About the Rainbow Kids Program

Impetus for the Program

I discovered early in my career as a primary teacher that the average child could master almost anything I could teach. No matter how lofty the concept or skill, if I can translate it into language that speaks to the youngster and present it in an engaging way, there's a good chance the child will get it. I also realized early on that many children seemed bored with the curriculum I was supposed to teach. They had mastered numbers and letters long ago by watching "Sesame Street" and were starved for the knowledge that real school had promised them.

I felt it my duty to deliver my headiest stuff. My shapes unit included pentagons, hexagons, and octagons. (Some eager customers even begged for dodecahedrons.) Our study of color turned the classroom into a messy laboratory of theorists, inventing and naming colors that hadn't been covered in preschool. The children weren't satisfied with our number line until we included infinity. And, when I asked them to suggest a topic of study, I was required to master dinosaurs. The longer the dinosaur's name, the better my students liked it.

In a world where nearly everyone looks down on you, these little people thrilled to discover that knowledge is indeed power. They'd swagger out the door at 2:30 armed with a juicy fact we had learned that day and rehearsed as the bell rang. "I'll bet you don't know how many bones are in the body?" they'd ask anyone who would listen. "Ha! 209!" I shunned teaching the upper grades. At no time is a child's love of learning more passionate—and teaching more fun—than in the early primary grades.

I had selfish reasons, too, for making learning fun. Classroom management had never been my strong suit and for some reason I always drew the most socially active children in the school, or so it seemed. I was continually challenged to keep the busy hum of activity from slipping into chaos. If I could distract the children from each other with a jazzy song or dramatic science lesson, I would have an easier time maintaining order—or so my theory went. I may have been my own worst enemy. Acting out the process of tooth decay, for example, probably stirred up more energy than I could manage in the classroom.

I faced the problem squarely. I asked for advice from experienced teachers with smoothly run classrooms. I attended workshops. I read books. I established rules and tried to follow through with consequences. I had lots of talks with the children. But even though students were good at giving me the right answers in discussion about "how we behave at school," pushing, yelling, and crying still punctuated the day.

I considered using more forceful means to bring the class under control. It wasn't in my nature, however, to threaten or punish. Scaring children into being good may work in the moment, but my own personal experience made me concerned about the long-term effects of fear tactics. As a child, I was intimidated by many of my teachers and often arrived at school with a tummy ache. I did everything I could to please the teacher and avoid disapproval. While I was mastering obedience, however, I was also learning to be docile, passive, and dependent. It took years of work as an adult to grow beyond the "good girl" role, find my voice, and take charge of my life. Surely there was a more respectful and effective way to help children get along with one another.

One day as I was preparing manipulatives for a math lesson, a thought crossed my mind. If I could make social concepts and feelings as concrete as counting bears, perhaps the children would have an easier time taking turns, cooperating, and solving their problems respectfully. The longer I thought about it, the more this notion grabbed me. What could be more abstract than the workings of human relations?

Consider this scenario: Kristin wants a marker, so she reaches across the table and takes one from the pile Sammy is using. This action causes Sammy to call her a thief and wrestle her to the ground to get it back. They both run to me and whine, "Sammy pushed me down!" "Kristin stole my marker!" Each child is only clear about what the other did wrong. Neither understands a personal role in contributing to the problem. Even the idea that an action led to a reaction is a concept too hefty for many young children.

Plus, it all happens so fast. Kristin and Sammy are on automatic pilot when it comes to getting what they want. The moment after Kristin decides she wants the marker, she has it in her hand. There is no time for Kristin to notice that the marker is sitting in front of Sammy or to consider how her taking it might upset him. Kristin's violation quickly elicits Sammy's hurtful response. How can Sammy come up with a better way to get the marker back in the nanosecond between Kristin's transgression and his knee-jerk reaction?

And what about the feelings that trigger their behavior? Kristin and Sammy can't see or smell or put a finger on the undercurrent of emotion that urges them to act. The feelings and needs of the other person are even more intangible. No wonder some of my students were stuck in negative behavior patterns. I had not translated these sophisticated concepts and skills into terms they could understand.

That's when I got the idea to write a story that makes these abstract notions concrete and easier for youngsters to grasp. The main characters in the story, a community of children, have suns that glow from the inside; the sunshine is externally visible when they are happy. In addition, their feelings are exhibited by the weather around them. Sunny weather corresponds with the pleasant range of emotion and cloudy weather represents uncomfortable feelings. So, for example, when the children are happy and content, their suns shine big and bright. When the children are kind to one another (*spreading sunshine*), their suns grow bigger than before. When the children experience unpleasant feelings, clouds appear in front of the suns and remain there until their feelings are experienced and released. When the children engage in hurtful behavior (*throwing clouds*), their clouds grow bigger. And finally, when the children learn to express their upsetting emotions in respectful ways, the problem gets solved, the clouds clear away, and their suns become visible again.

A weather image is also the source of the name for this special group of children. It often rains in the valley where they live, and whenever it does, they enjoy dancing and playing in the rain. As the light from the children's suns shines through the raindrops, rainbows appear around them, thus their name—the rainbow kids.

The story line carries the characters through a series of episodes in which their actions, skillful and unskillful, result in visible changes in the weather. As students hear the story they discover that feelings are real, though they ordinarily can't be seen, that feelings change, and that the way they treat one another can affect everyone.

The Rainbow Kids Learn To Talk It Out

Like any good teaching tool, the *Rainbow Kids Program* has taken years to refine. My initial instincts were right. The rainbows, suns, and clouds were enormously appealing to children and effective in making their feelings concrete. After hearing the story, they could more easily identify and talk about their feelings using the simple *sunny* and *cloudy* descriptors. The children loved the weather cutouts and began drawing their feelings into artwork by adding suns and clouds.

When our attention shifted away to other things, however, the concepts were soon forgotten. To solidify the children's identification with the characters and deepen their understanding of the concepts embedded in the story, I rewrote the story for 24 characters and put the names of my students in the text. When we talked about the concepts after that, they only needed to consult their vicarious experience of the kids' adventures.

I also followed the presentation of the story with lessons specifically designed to show children how suns and clouds relate to their lives. (Follow-up lessons and activities are presented in Part II.) Once children saw the connection between the weather metaphors in the story and their own emotional experiences, they were better able to apply the new ideas in real life. I distinctly remember the moment when that first rainbow kid, a child who habitually struck back when provoked, ran to me and reported that someone had *thrown a cloud* at him. "How do I *clear it away* again?" he asked. The teachable moment had arrived.

It is embarrassing today to recall my early response to that question: I told him to brush the cloud aside. Why? Because that is what I had always done when confronted with an unpleasant social situation. Fortunately, I did not offer this advice for long. One of the parents of a rainbow kid suggested I present children with options other than avoidance and I realized the importance of teaching more sophisticated responses.

My search for more effective ways of handling conflict led me to the Peninsula Conflict Resolution Center, a neighborhood dispute mediation program. Coincidentally, they had begun to expand their services to schools and were looking for someone to direct their new program. I was eventually offered the job and for the next three years immersed myself in the field of conflict resolution.

The formal training I received in mediation and negotiation answered my questions about how to resolve conflicts more skillfully. But I was unable to find a program that would help teachers to help young children resolve their conflicts. I had the knowledge I needed, however, to create

the program myself. Bringing together my fourteen years of classroom teaching experience and my newly learned conflict resolution skills, I created *Talk It Out*, a teacher-friendly approach for teaching peacemaking skills to elementary students. Since the publication of my book, *Talk It Out: Conflict Resolution in the Elementary Classroom* (Porro, 1996), I have trained thousands of teachers nationwide in the art of turning tattled tales into problem-solving opportunities.

The *Rainbow Kids Program* deepened immeasurably with my new understanding about conflict resolution. Instead of passing on my dysfunctional approach of brushing problems aside, I could now teach children to *clear clouds away* by talking about feelings, listening respectfully, and finding solutions that work for everyone involved. Since refining the *Rainbow Kids Program*, I have worked with hundreds of teachers who have used the ideas to teach their students about *suns, clouds,* and *clearing clouds away.* Their experiences, feedback, and insights have deepened the program as well.

Differences Between *Rainbow Kids* and *Talk It Out*

Although the *Rainbow Kids* and the *Talk It Out* programs evolved together and are designed to teach the same conflict resolution concepts and skills, there are distinct differences between the programs. *Talk It Out* focuses on teaching elementary children a four-step process for solving their social problems—cool off, talk and listen to each other, brainstorm solutions, and choose the idea you like best. When implemented schoolwide, *Talk It Out* establishes a common goal and provides the entire school community with a common language for handling disagreements respectfully.

The *Rainbow Kids Program* translates these same conflict resolution strategies into language young children can easily grasp. When conflicts arise, children are taught to *clear the clouds away* using the same steps described in *Talk It Out.* Children exposed to the *Rainbow Kids Program* in the early grades can easily advance to an upper grade classroom that uses *Talk It Out.*

In addition to teaching problem-solving skills, the *Rainbow Kids Program* also teaches emotional literacy and social skills outside the context of conflict. Children are taught to be self-aware when they have positive feelings and to extend their feelings to others. They learn how to openly care about and empathize with others' feelings. Children also discover how their actions affect them and those around them. When children truly understand the relationship between their actions and what follows, they are able to make better choices about how to treat others.

The story used to introduce the program also teaches children how to create a warm, caring community and summons their commitment to do so. How this occurs can best be illustrated by recalling what happened to Raymond.

Raymond Meets the Rainbow Kids

Raymond was transferred into my 1st grade class in March, a smooth-sailing time of year when most of the kinks had been ironed out and the *Rainbow Kids Program* was in full swing. Before Raymond's first day, we imagined how it might feel to be "the new kid" so late in the school year and talked about ways we could *spread sunshine* to Raymond to help him feel welcome. By the time Raymond arrived, the children were so enthusiastic about their plans that I had to delay the morning lessons until everyone had a chance to greet Raymond, show him around the room, and give him a tour of the school. Raymond had no trouble receiving the positive attention. Indeed, he seemed to eat it up.

By Raymond's second week, however, the honeymoon was over and an angry Raymond emerged. When Raymond made a mistake, he balled up his paper and threw it. If someone got too close to his seat, he'd spit and yell. At the slightest provocation, Raymond flew into a rage, toppling desks and running out of the room. I later learned that the baseball cap he always wore concealed bald patches on his head—since his father had left home, Raymond had been tearing out his hair.

Needless to say, we were all thrown into a tizzy when this formidable force blew into the room. One by one the children came to me and insisted that I tell Raymond the story, as if knowledge about *suns* and *clouds* would somehow fix his rage. I thought this was a good idea, but I was thoroughly preoccupied with helping Raymond manage his anger. Each time he lost control, I walked, or rather wrestled, him to the time-out seat in the back of the room and left him with these words: "As soon as you are in control, you are welcome to return."

Over the next week I spent a great deal of time watching Raymond lose his temper; restraining Raymond; struggling with him to the time-out seat;

inviting him back; and waiting for the cycle to begin again. The other students had a routine, too. Each time Raymond had an outburst, they'd quickly let me know what happened and take giant steps backward to get out of the way of the storm. Their worried faces seemed to say, "He doesn't understand." During calmer moments, a few brave children continued to approach Raymond and say something nice or offer help. I had not cued them to continue *spreading sunshine*. They were reaching out to Raymond on their own.

School life continued like this for a couple weeks. The other children and I continued to use the language of the rainbow kids, talking about *spreading sunshine* and *clearing the clouds away*. At one point, I realized that although Raymond's outbursts seemed as frequent as the day before, he no longer wrestled with me as I escorted him to the time-out seat and he didn't stay there as long as before because he began to bring his aggressive impulses under control more quickly. Still later, he was able to walk there by himself at my verbal request.

It was around this time that the miracle began to happen. One afternoon a child excitedly raced to me and announced loud enough for everyone to hear, "Raymond just *spread sunshine!*" The children spontaneously jumped to their feet and clapped and cheered for Raymond, who sheepishly smiled from his seat.

The next morning was Raymond's. He systematically went from one child to another, saying or doing something kind, with only occasional breaks to consult a wad of paper stuffed in his pocket. Apparently he had written down everyone's name and the kind gestures he had planned. "He's *spreading sunshine!*" rang out again and again, followed by more claps and cheers.

From that day on, Raymond was one of the kids. His intense emotions did not disappear, but now when they hit, he ran to the time-out seat, waited for the anger to pass, and returned to his desk without a word from me. A short time later, his mother came to school and asked what was happening. She had never seen Raymond so excited about school. At his last school, she reported, it had been a struggle to get him up and dressed each morning. (It was a private school with a spiritual focus, and he eventually was asked to leave because he didn't fit in.) Now Raymond could hardly wait to get to school each morning.

In all my years of teaching, I had never seen a child make such a profound and rapid shift from negative to positive behavior. I credit the rainbow kids in my class. They never stopped caring about Raymond, even in the midst of all those *clouds*. They never *threw the clouds back* and escalated the hostility, even when Raymond was hurtful to them. They never lost sight of the loving community they were seeking to create. And when that alluringly loving community was held out to Raymond, he wanted so much to belong that he figured out how to change. He taught himself to manage his anger in order to maximize time with the other students. In fact, I was lucky enough to teach a 1st and 2nd grade multiage class that year and I looped with the 1st graders. Raymond was one of the most positive leaders in the 2nd grade class the following year.

As I tried to identify the factors that had contributed to Raymond's turn-around, I realized that the students had learned something from *The Rainbow Kids Story* that I had not explicitly taught—that it is possible to live together in a caring community where everyone belongs, everyone is loved, and problems are handled respectfully. The story not only established a vision of how we look, feel, and act in such a community, but secured commitment on the students' part to make it happen, a commitment so strong that even Raymond could not pull them off track. The loving environment they established exceeded my every expectation of what was possible.

What happened to Raymond in my class compelled me to write this book. My students had proved two profound things to me: Love really does have the power to transform; and given a clear vision and the tools to create it, children can lead the way.

Overview of the Program

The *Rainbow Kids Program* has the same three components you will find in any good lesson: an introduction, specific skill instruction, and opportunities for practice.

Introduction to the program's key concepts is accomplished by reading *The Rainbow Kids Story* aloud to students. The story uses concrete weather metaphors to heighten children's awareness of their feelings and the choices they have about how to express them.

Skill instruction occurs through a series of seven lessons that relate the metaphors to children's personal experience and promote specific social and emotional learning.

Practice opportunities arise spontaneously in the course of day-to-day classroom life. Tips for recognizing and taking advantage of these teachable moments, as well as suggestions for more formal practice, are also provided in the lessons.

The book is divided into three main parts and Appendixes.

Part I discusses the concepts and skills presented in the program, and provides a guide to *The Rainbow Kids Story* and a detailed description of how to implement the program with students. *The Rainbow Kids Story* is reproduced (with sample students' names) in Part I.

Part II contains the instructional component of the program—lessons and activities that teach specific social skills. Each lesson includes a list of objectives, procedures for presenting the lessons, notes related to the lesson's content, and ideas for extension and follow-up activities.

The Appendixes contain resources and materials for implementing the program, including master copies of the weather symbols. A poster, facilitator's guide, and sample parent letter are also provided in this section.

Part III is the booklet that contains the master copy of *The Rainbow Kids Story*. For your convenience, the story is also available online at http://www.ascd.org/rainbowkids. You may download the electronic file and insert your students' names, as appropriate, and edit the story to use in your classroom.

Limitations of the Program

The most appealing characteristic of the *Rainbow Kids Program* may also be its greatest limitation. Since the program is easy enough for youngsters to understand, it is necessarily simplistic in its presentation of human emotion and behavior. So, while the program introduces young students to some fairly sophisticated generalizations about feelings and interpersonal relations, it is only useful as far as it goes. *The Rainbow Kids Story* and the weather metaphors are not intended to communicate the full complexity of human experience.

It should also be noted that, while the *cloudy* term is used as a general descriptor for a range of unpleasant emotions, the program only explores feelings that accompany the "garden variety" conflicts that occur in most classrooms. Children who feel angry, frustrated, and hurt when classmates tease, take things, don't share, tell secrets, bug, and argue will surely benefit from learning how to *clear clouds away*. There may be heavier *clouds* in your classroom, however, that will not dissipate so easily. Children with special needs or children who are experiencing difficult psychological states—such as depression or loss—will need the support of professional help.

▶   ▶   ▶   ▶   ▶

Why the Program Works

When I first began using *Rainbow Kids* with my students, I was surprised at how well it worked. After a decade of searching for ways to help students with problem behaviors, I had found something that changed children before my very eyes. It felt like magic. Anyone who has been held captive in a classroom inhabited by a few children stuck in dysfunctional behavior patterns can appreciate the thrill. Not only did it work for me, it worked for others. Teachers who have implemented the program report similar results:

▶ My children love the story and are very earnest about becoming rainbow kids. It works like magic.

▶ *Rainbow Kids* is especially effective with my aggressive children who have limited language skills. They are much more aware of feelings and now they can talk about them as well.

▶ *Rainbow Kids* helps me stay focused on the positive. When children tattle, I calmly validate their feelings and ask them how they want to deal with the *clouds*. I am amazed by their ideas.

My friends who are English teachers tell me that the *Rainbow Kids Program* is effective because it uses two powerful literary devices—story-telling and metaphor. In my work as a staff developer, I am often reminded of the power of narrative to grab and educate the listener. My conflict resolution workshop, which I have presented for more than 10 years, opens with a story about a nasty problem I had with a neighbor. The story ends well, of course, due to the "talk it out" skills I was able to use. When I return to schools where I presented the workshop, teachers pull me aside and tell me about a recent problem with an upset parent or spouse or friend. "I remembered what you did with your neighbor," they report. "It really helped." They don't mention the posters, the handouts, or the activities they experienced in the other five hours of the workshop. It was the story that stuck with them and came through when they needed it.

In her course, Translating Brain Research into Instructional Practice, Pat Wolfe explains that storytelling and metaphor take advantage of how the brain learns best. The brain easily remembers stories because, unlike random or unconnected data, stories have a beginning, middle, and end. Stories are also evocative and relevant to students, two essential characteristics because the brain only stores information that is meaningful and contains an emotional hook. *The Rainbow Kids Story* is especially good at "hooking" students because they "play" the characters in the story.

Metaphor, on the other hand, is effective because it fastens new information to information that is already stored in the brain. The lessons about feelings in *The Rainbow Kids Story* are conveniently linked to children's everyday experience of weather.

Psychologists who have reviewed the program suggest that it is effective because it teaches students how to change as opposed to lecturing them about how to behave. Although I had extensive training in Gestalt therapy years before developing *Rainbow Kids*, I did not purposefully use my knowledge about psychology in my work with students. I realize now that as I learned and changed, so did my teaching. I had inadvertently incorporated into the program what I had internalized in my personal life about the process of change.

Change Begins with Self-Awareness

According to Gestalt psychology, change takes place when we become aware of what we are already doing, not when we try to make a change (Korb, Gorrell, & Van De Riet, 1989). The Gestalt theory of change emphasizes the importance of being self-aware. Self-awareness is the ability to pay attention to what is happening more closely than we ordinarily do. Usually we are so caught up in experience that we do not realize what we are feeling, thinking, and doing at the time. When we become self-aware, we establish a parallel stream of consciousness where we can notice what is happening as it occurs.

How does self-awareness lead to growth? To give an example, I'll describe a personal problem I struggled with for years—the challenge of finding time for myself. I have always been a busy person, both socially and in my work as a teacher. After long hours at school, I would habitually get caught up in the social lives of my housemates and friends. I valued quiet, introspective time, but weeks often slipped by with no chance to relax, read, or do something nurturing for myself.

I blamed my hectic pace on life in general, those circumstances beyond my control. Teaching was demanding. No matter how many hours I put in, I found I was continuously preoccupied with planning the next school day. My friends sometimes seemed too demanding. Our conversations often centered on my helping them through a crisis. Although I enjoyed being a trusted confidant, I sometimes resented how much time and attention they seemed to require.

It wasn't until I brought the issue to my Gestalt therapy group that I was able to see the problem differently. The work of change began by my entertaining the possibility that I was responsible for creating a life that did not include time for myself, a ludicrous idea at first. My therapist suggested that

I study the problem from an objective perspective, that I continue doing everything exactly the same way, but this time with awareness.

As I had already established an "observer-self" for other self-improvement projects, it was just a question of focusing attention on this new problem area. Now when I socialized or got caught up in school work, my observer-self kept me posted about what I was feeling, thinking, and doing. So, for example, when the phone rang, I watched myself run to pick it up. Upon hearing the friend's voice, I noticed how trapped I felt by the thought, "This will cost at least half an hour."

Although I wasn't able to be this mindful all the time, a few moments of truth went a long way toward informing me about how I created my problem. I had the unconscious, well-established habit of putting everyone's needs ahead of my own. In fact, before this exercise, I wasn't even aware that I had any needs, outside my overriding desire to meet the needs of others, which was also unconscious. If I was serious about finding time for myself, I would have to get serious about taking that time.

Self-Awareness Opens Up Opportunities for Change

It's a short but difficult step from identifying the need to change to doing something about it. Armed with information about how I gave my time away, I was better prepared to interrupt the old habit and reserve space for me. That may sound simple, but it did not happen overnight. At first, the best I could do was catch myself after the fact. For example, after a 45-minute phone call, I would notice there was no time for the walk I'd planned. Doing the same old thing with awareness, however, was a step up from unconscious behavior. With that awareness, I would answer the phone, but be "in a hurry" because of a previous commitment. Or, I might not answer the phone at all. Still later I found my own apartment and bought an answering machine.

This experience and others like it taught me that change takes place when I pay attention to what I am feeling, thinking, and doing, and when I notice how my actions affect me and those around me. It then becomes obvious that I have chosen to act in a particular way and am therefore responsible for what is happening to me. Finally, I open up to the possibility of making a different choice, of acting in a way that works better. Heightened self-awareness creates compelling opportunities to act in more satisfying ways.

The *Rainbow Kids Program* teaches these same awareness concepts through the weather metaphors. The concepts include awareness of self (thoughts, feelings, and actions), awareness of choices about how to act, and awareness of the consequences of each of those choices (see Note). The *sunny* and *cloudy* metaphors heighten children's awareness of their feelings. The *spreading sunshine* metaphor points out that when we choose to act in caring ways, the outcome is often favorable (e.g., the suns of both the giver and the receiver get bigger in *The Rainbow Kids Story*). When upsetting emotions are expressed in hurtful or disrespectful ways (*throwing clouds*), neither person gets what they truly need. (The clouds get bigger for both.) And, when upsets are expressed respectfully, problems can often be solved in ways that satisfy everyone (the *clouds clear away*). These concepts and the corresponding weather metaphors are summarized in Figure 2.1.

> *Note:* Although the Rainbow Kids program is not specifically designed to heighten children's awareness of their thoughts, how children habitually think about events leads to either a fundamentally optimistic or a fundamentally pessimistic view of reality, which in turn affects children's feelings and actions. This topic, along with suggestions for teaching children the cognitive skills of optimism, is fully explored in *The Optimistic Child* (Seligman, 1995).

FIGURE 2.1
AWARENESS CONCEPTS IN THE *RAINBOW KIDS PROGRAM*

Symbol	Develops awareness of	Children learn
Feeling *sunny*	Feelings	Sometimes I feel happy.
Spreading sunshine	Choice	When I feel happy, I can extend those feelings to others.
	Consequence	When I openly care about others, we both tend to feel happy.*
	Consequence	When I give to others, they are likely to give to me in return. *
Feeling *cloudy*	Feelings	Sometimes I feel angry, upset, or unhappy.
	Choice	When I feel hurt, I can hurt others in return.
Throwing clouds	Consequence	When I hurt others, the problem often gets bigger for everyone.*
	Consequence	When I hurt others, I am likely to be hurt in return.*
	Consequence	When I hurt others, it can be difficult for me to get what I really need.*
Clearing clouds away	Choice	When I am upset, I can help myself feel better.
	Choice	When I am upset with someone, I can talk to the person about the problem and look for solutions we both like.
	Consequence	When I solve problems in respectful ways, we both feel better. Everyone wins.*

* Although the consequences described are generally true, these outcomes are tentatively stated because it is not possible to predict how another person will respond. If, for example, you offered me encouragement (*spread sunshine*) at a time when I felt cynical, I might become irritated rather than feel supported. So, while it is useful to teach children that kindness and respect are generally appreciated by others and often lead to positive outcomes, paying attention to what really happens as a result of our actions and learning from that outcome, is the larger lesson.

Feelings Are Personal and Changeable

The rainbow kids' special ability to display their emotions teaches students that feelings are real and that each of us has emotional responses. Having a physical reminder that different people may feel differently about the same thing is an important concept for children. Although the children in your classroom do not have suns and clouds broadcasting their feelings, they will engage with that concept while the weather icons are being held up in class. The practice can help them understand that Edgar may enjoy chasing Katrina on the playground, for example, while Katrina may not like that game.

The weather symbols also dramatically demonstrate that feelings change over time. Just because James is frustrated right now doesn't mean he will be frustrated all day. In his book, *The Optimistic Child* (1995), Seligman notes that children who understand that bad moods are temporary and changeable are more likely to bounce back from setbacks and resist depression than children who view bad moods as lasting and permanent.

The changing weather symbols help students learn the concept that people may like different things at different times. While Mandy enjoyed playing with Hannah this morning, Mandy may want to play with someone else this afternoon and again with Hannah tomorrow.

Finally, the weather metaphors demonstrate that, like the real sun and clouds, feelings are not right or wrong, good or bad, they just are. And, like real weather, feelings come and go on their own, uninvited by us.

Children Can Recognize and Label Feelings

As children identify with the rainbow kids and watch their emotional climate change, they are encouraged to tune in to their own experiences and share their feelings with others. The *sunny* and *cloudy* descriptors provide children with a simple, beginning vocabulary for labeling pleasant and unpleasant emotions. Later, in the follow-up activities, children are encouraged to go beyond the simple *sunny* and *cloudy* terms and learn feeling words that describe the full range of emotions. According to many experts in the field of emotional intelligence (Stone-McCowen, Jensen, Freedman, & Rideout, 1998; Hawkins & Catalano 1992; Greenberg, Kusche, Cook, & Quamma, 1995; Goleman 1995; Elias et al., 1997; and others) recognizing and naming one's emotions is a key skill in developing emotional literacy.

Feelings and Actions Are Different

Young students tend to experience a feeling and act upon it quickly, therefore it is important to slow this process down and help them understand that feelings and actions are not the same thing. Feelings arise on their own and give us important information about what is going on inside us. What we do with those feelings, the action we take, is a matter of choice. Understanding this distinction can be difficult, especially for people who tend to act impulsively. Indeed, children who automatically react to emotional situations may not realize they are making a choice or that other responses are even possible.

Feelings and actions are differentiated in *The Rainbow Kids Story*. First the kids experience a feeling in the form of a cloud or sun, then they choose a response *(spread sunshine, throw clouds, or clear clouds away)*. Separating feelings from actions teaches children that they, too, have a choice about how they react to emotional situations and encourages them to make a thoughtful response. The ability to consciously choose how to respond to an emotion is another important skill in the development of emotional intelligence.

Actions Have Consequences

The dynamic weather symbols are especially effective in helping children see that actions lead to predictable outcomes and that some outcomes are more favorable than others. When the kids *throw clouds back* (retaliate), for example, children notice that *clouds* get bigger and upsetting feelings tend to increase. When the kids work to solve problems in respectful ways, everyone feels satisfied and the *clouds clear away*. As children watch the rainbow kids' symbols change in response to their actions, they learn how their own actions affect others, both positively and negatively. With that knowledge they are more inclined to choose actions that have a positive impact on everyone.

Conflicts Can Be Resolved Respectfully

The turning point in *The Rainbow Kids Story* comes when Julie and
Dennis, two of the kids, figure out how to resolve their conflict in a way
that works for them both (they *clear their clouds away*). This example
teaches students that when social problems arise, they can manage their
upsetting feelings and assert themselves in respectful ways, empathize with
others' concerns, and find solutions that satisfy everyone.

The conflict resolution skills taught in the lessons include cooling off,
speaking and listening respectfully, brainstorming solutions, and selecting

what works best. Once children become acquainted with these skills, they are encouraged to practice them when real-life problems occur.

Create a Caring, Respectful Classroom Community

Empathy and consideration of others is another idea promoted in the program. The rainbow kids value positive social behavior and model how to show caring toward one other *(spread sunshine)*. This idea is further emphasized when the kids' suns shine through raindrops to produce rainbows, a dazzling display of their positive emotional capacity. At the end of the story the kids also discover that their suns are always available to them. Even when angry or upset, they can choose to relate to one another from their essential caring nature, for example, by *clearing clouds away* (see Note).

> *Note:* Every educational program is based upon a particular view of human nature. I believe that children are basically caring and compassionate and are most likely to exhibit these qualities when they are trusted to do so. If children act in thoughtless ways it is because they are missing information and skills. Our job as teachers is to provide them with the guidance they need to become caring classmates and effective problem solvers. This optimistic view of children is drawn from my own teaching experiences and supported by leading researchers in the field of child development. This research is extensively reviewed in Alfie Kohn's *The Brighter Side of Human Nature: Altruism and Empathy in Everyday Life* (1990).

As children vicariously experience the kindness the rainbow kids show one another, they identify this same caring capacity within themselves. The respectful community the kids establish in Rainbow Valley demonstrates to children that, if they look beyond themselves, they can choose behaviors that not only satisfy their own needs but also contribute to the well-being of the classroom community.

The Payoff

The rewards of teaching these concepts and skills are great. When we approach social and emotional learning with as much attention as we devote to traditional subjects, problem behaviors decrease, the quality of relationships in the classroom improves, and academic achievement increases (Elias et al., 1997). According to Daniel Goleman (1995), studies show again and again that emotional literacy programs enhance schools' ability to teach. Children who can handle their upsets, control their impulses, and focus their attention are more available to learn reading, writing, and math. Children who feel important and cared about are also more likely to care about others and fully invest in the school experience. Beyond these educational advantages, social and emotional learning seems to help children develop better friendships, grow up to be better parents and colleagues, and become responsible, contributing members of society.

Social and emotional education benefits teachers as well. Teaching in a classroom where children are socially competent is fun and supports me to do my best work and thrive right along with the children. It also fulfills my purpose in becoming a teacher—I make a significant difference in the lives of my students.

▷ ▷ ▷ ▷ ▷

3

A Guide to *The Rainbow Kids Story*

The Rainbow Kids Story, the centerpiece of the program, serves as a vehicle for introducing children to the key concepts of the program (see Figure 2.1, p. 24). Each kid in the story is equipped with a personal weather system that broadcasts feelings and changes with each passing emotion. As the story is told, suns and clouds of different sizes are held up to correspond with the kids' feelings. Pleasant feelings manifest as suns; the more elevated the emotion, the bigger the sun. Unpleasant feelings cover the sun with a cloud; the more intense the emotion, the bigger the cloud. As the kids interact and cause each other's weather to change, your students learn to identify feelings and the changes that result from different behaviors. In this way, students actually see and understand how their actions affect themselves and those around them.

This story guide will further acquaint you with the concepts presented in *The Rainbow Kids Story*. The guide summarizes the story and discusses each weather symbol and the concept it is designed to teach. It will also help familiarize you with the story's plot and characters and prepare you to present the story to your students.

The story itself appears at the end of this chapter with sample student names in it. (The same names are used in the following summary.) When you present the story to your students, replace these sample names with their names. A complete story "script" with blanks to fill with your students' names is provided in a separate booklet at the end of this book. For your convenience, it is also appears online at http://www.ascd.org /rainbowkids. You may download the file, fill in the blanks with your students' names, modify personal pronouns appropriately, as well as modify the story itself.

The Rainbow Kids Story, Part I

Introduction

The story begins with narration introducing us to the rainbow kids, a community of children who have the unusual inherent ability to communicate their feelings through weather symbols. In the first part of the story the children are happy, caring, and respectful of one another. Their suns, therefore, shine brightly much of the time. The *sunny* term is used to describe a range of pleasant emotions that are likely to be present whenever basic needs are satisfied. Happy, glad, excited, grateful, loving, generous, and joyous might all be categorized as *sunny* feelings. The *sunny* metaphor helps children differentiate and label positive emotions in themselves and others and heightens their self-awareness whenever they feel happy.

Mildly unhappy feelings also visit the kids in the first part of the story. Whenever the kids experience upsetting emotions, clouds appear in front of their suns. The clouds represent emotions that accompany unmet needs and include such feelings as disappointment, sadness, anger, hurt, and frustration. The *cloudy* metaphor helps children identify and label unpleasant feelings in themselves and others.

The story's opening narrative also explains how the kids got their name. If often rains in the valley where the kids live, and whenever it does, they dance and play in the rain. As their suns shine through the raindrops, the sky lights up with rainbows. The kids get their nickname from these rainbows: the rainbow kids. Their ability to create the full spectrum of color is the ultimate display of their capacity to care.

Scenes 1, 2, and 3: The Picnic, Marble Spill, and Surprise Party

Caring about others is a favorite pastime in Part I of the story when the kids are so happy. *Spreading sunshine*, as the kids call it, is any expression of goodwill toward another. Three vignettes—the Picnic, the Marble Spill, and the Surprise Party—show the kids actively seeking ways to openly care about their friends either by word or deed. Here students discover that when they feel happy, one of the choices available to them is to extend their feelings to others. Each time a kid *spreads sunshine* to another, both the giver and the receiver end up with bigger suns. Often the child who initiates the kindness is offered kindness in return. By watching the kids' suns grow with each thoughtful gesture, children learn that when *sunny* emotions are openly expressed, positive feelings tend to grow, and what they give to others they are likely to receive in return.

In each of the three vignettes, the kids also experience a few cloudy moments when sadness or disappointment occurs. The kids respond to these situations by either solving the problem at hand or by *spreading sunshine* to the upset child to help him feel better. The kids' relatively simple approach to dealing with unpleasant emotions corresponds to their limited experience with upsetting events.

Scene 4: A Sad Story and a Bright Idea

In this scene we hear about Zeke, an unhappy child who lives alone in a cave not far from the valley. Although the kids have never seen Zeke, they've heard stories about him and are bothered that he lives in a dark place without friends or sunshine. One day, a couple of the kids, Audrey and Jasper, decide to leave the valley and search for Zeke in an effort to *spread sunshine* to him. The first night out, the two kids camp near Zeke's cave, though they don't realize it because the cave is hidden behind a bush. Zeke, however, hears their voices and creeps to the front of the cave to get a closer look. He sees the sleeping children and notices the light shining from their covers. Zeke looks down at himself and sees that he is surrounded by clouds. Zeke's clouds correspond to the unhappy feelings that accompany his unmet needs. As a socially isolated child, Zeke has no chance to feel important or cared about.

The next morning, Audrey and Jasper wake up, pack their bags, and set off to continue their search for Zeke. When the kids disappear, Zeke becomes curious, and peeks outside the cave to investigate. Instead of finding the two kids, however, he discovers little rainbows dancing in the misty valley below. Part I ends as Zeke makes his way into the valley to find out what the rainbow lights are all about.

The Rainbow Kids Story, Part II

Scene 5: Zeke Meets the Rainbow Kids

Luis is the first rainbow kid to see Zeke when he arrives in the valley. Luis welcomes the newcomer by offering an apple. But Zeke, who lacks empathy and social skills, grabs Luis's apple, pushes him aside, and runs away. Luis cries out, and a cloud appears in front of his sun. Here Zeke introduces *throwing clouds*, the metaphor for unkind behaviors that hurt others emotionally or physically. *Throwing clouds* is Zeke's unskillful way of getting what he wants. Zeke takes the apple without considering how Luis will be affected.

Another unhealthy way of handling difficult emotions (though this is not illustrated in the story) is to hide feelings and withdraw. When children become overly passive or blame themselves when things go wrong, they are, in effect, *throwing clouds* at themselves. Like aggressive children, they too must learn to express feelings in ways that lead to more positive outcomes.

Luis's cries attract the attention of Hannah, another rainbow kid, who rushes to comfort him. The kids are confused by Zeke's hurtful behavior and decide to follow the boy and attempt to make friends with him. When they come to a water fountain, however, they find Erin sitting on the ground, also looking cloudy. Zeke had shoved her out of the way so he could get a drink. They help Erin to her feet and continue walking in the direction Zeke had run.

Meanwhile, Zeke has arrived at a park where the rest of the kids are playing. As Zeke watches, he becomes intrigued by the children's happy faces. He decides it must be the toys that make the kids smile and, in an effort to be happy like them, runs through the park collecting their playthings.

By the time Luis, Hannah, and Erin catch up with Zeke, he is heading out of the valley, loaded with toys. Although the three attempt to stop him, Zeke doubles his speed and quickly scurries up the hill and back to his cave. He dumps the toys in a corner and waits for them to make him happy. When the toys have no effect, Zeke angrily kicks them, curls up under a cloud, and falls asleep.

Everything changes for the kids that day. Even after Zeke departs, clouds still cover the kids and make it hard for them to see their suns. Once the kids lose touch with their light, their happy feelings are replaced by fear and confusion. Instead of caring about others, they yell, grab, and push. With each hurtful action come bigger clouds. Before long there is no caring, no light; when it rains there are no rainbows.

This cloudy episode dramatically demonstrates how hurtful actions escalate hostile feelings, increase quarrelsome behavior, and bring about sadness and isolation. Each time feelings are expressed in aggressive ways, the problem grows bigger and the outcome is disastrous for everyone.

Scene 6: The Dazzling Duo Meets Zeke

Meanwhile Audrey and Jasper, who have grown tired looking for Zeke, give up the search and retrace their steps toward home. They reach the last hill as it begins to rain, recognize the place they had camped the first night, and decide to stay there again. In their search for shelter, they discover the cave behind the bush. They enter, unroll their sleeping bags near the front of the cave, and fall asleep.

Zeke recognizes the kids at once and watches from his cloudy corner to again try to discover what makes them happy. After the kids fall asleep, he creeps to the front of the cave. As Zeke comes closer to the kids and their light, his skin begins to warm. Zeke likes the warm feeling and figures out it must be the light that makes the kids happy. He tries to scoop some up, but when it slips through his fingers, he decides to take one of the kids back to his cloudy corner. Zeke spends the rest of the night sleeping next to Jasper's warm glow.

In the morning, Jasper stirs and discovers himself next to Zeke—who is hugging him—in the back of the cave. When Audrey hears that Zeke has been found, she gives a cheer. Her shout, however, startles Zeke, and he retreats deeper into a corner. Jasper attempts to gain Zeke's trust, but his efforts are in vain. Zeke shows no signs of understanding and continues to look at Jasper suspiciously. When words don't work to communicate, Audrey suggests they show Zeke what they mean by filling his cave with light. Part II concludes as Audrey races down the hill to ask her rainbow friends to help light up the cave. Jasper stays behind and continues to *spread sunshine* to Zeke.

The Rainbow Kids Story, Part III

Scene 7: The Hide and Seek Game

Audrey realizes something is wrong when she reaches the cloudy valley. She searches for the kids and discovers them playing hide-and-seek in the park. She watches the action from a distance. Julie, who is "it," finishes counting and, after a quick look around, finds Dennis under a picnic table. Julie calls Dennis "out," and Dennis angrily accuses her of cheating. Julie returns the insult by calling Dennis's hiding place "dumb." Dennis counters with more hurtful words, and so the argument builds. Each time Julie and Dennis retaliate, the cloud sailing between them grows larger.

Dennis and Julie's actions are typical of children who respond to conflicts aggressively. When someone hurts them, their automatic reaction is to hurt the other person back. Like Julie and Dennis, they act without finding out more about what happened or thinking about the best way to handle the situation. Children who impulsively retaliate are also not aware of the negative consequences of their actions. The argument between Julie and Dennis unfolds slowly enough for children to see how "getting someone back" only increases hostility and the likelihood that more hurtful behavior will be returned.

As Audrey watches Julie and Dennis, she realizes that each time one tries to hurt the other, the cloud returns bigger than before. Audrey decides to act, and, with arms outstretched, walks between the two and shouts for them to stop. The kids in hiding hear Audrey and warn her to run from the

clouds, but it is too late. All the clouds are sailing straight toward her. Through a series of steps and turns, Audrey pirouettes around the clouds, which float by and eventually settle around Julie and Dennis.

The kids are amazed to discover that Audrey is still sunny after standing in the middle of a storm. Audrey explains that the clouds had nothing to do with her, so she stepped out of their way. Jameil figures out that clouds stick to clouds, and because Audrey is so sunny, the clouds have nothing to stick to.

Here Audrey stumbles upon a response that an emotionally intelligent person might consciously make. Instead of engaging in the battle or running away, she side-steps the hurtful behavior and looks for ways to move the action in a more positive direction. Although it might be difficult for most children (and adults) to remain calm and think clearly in the face of such adversity, Audrey, from her child-like perspective, innocently intuits her way through this scene and the one that follows.

The conversation continues as the kids try to figure out how to deal with their clouds. Audrey suggests they *clear the clouds away* and shows them how by helping Dennis and Julie solve their hide-and-seek problem. The *clearing clouds away* metaphor introduces children to the possibility of expressing their upsets in ways that lead to positive outcomes. *Clearing clouds away* requires children to care about each other even in the face of conflict, to communicate their needs and feelings respectfully, and to seek solutions that work for everyone. As Dennis and Julie's *clouds clear away*, children discover that when conflicts are approached with care, everyone wins and friendly (*sunny*) feelings return.

Next Lizzy notices that Jasper is missing. Her comment elicits Audrey's story about finding Zeke and needing the kids to help light the cave and communicate their message of friendship. The kids, most of whom are still cloudy, express their doubts about having a sun. Audrey tries to convince them that their suns are still shining behind the clouds. When the kids remain skeptical, Audrey invites them to go with her to Zeke's cave and see for themselves. The kids agree to accompany her in an effort to be helpful.

Scene 8: The Grand Finale

Audrey leads the kids up the path and into Zeke's cave. The kids' gesture to help Audrey and Jasper is enough to make their suns visible inside the darkness. The kids smile at the sight of their suns, making their suns grow bigger. As their suns fill the cave with light, the clouds melt away and Zeke warms up. Zeke relaxes and smiles as he realizes the kids are offering him the gift of happiness, which he was seeking all along. Theresa notices a tiny spot glowing in the center of Zeke's chest and announces that even he has a sun.

As the kids prepare to return home, Jasper extends his hand to Zeke, who eagerly takes it. Audrey leads the way out of the cave and, as it begins to rain, a line of rainbows marches down the hill. The most special rainbow is the little one at the end, holding hands with Jasper.

The story concludes by pointing out that the kids never lost their capacity to care, even when they were covered with clouds and forgot how to *spread sunshine*. Their positive sense of self was restored as soon as they started caring about each other. Even Zeke, the most troubled character in the story, has the same caring capacity at his core.

Epilogue

In this short concluding passage, the narrator talks about the changes that occurred in the valley after the kids returned with their new friend Zeke. Zeke learned to talk and to ask for what he wanted instead of grabbing. He also learned to *spread sunshine* and appreciate the warm feelings that accompany kind gestures.

The rainbow kids learned from Zeke as well. They learned that no matter what the weather, their caring nature is always intact. Of course, the kids still became angry at times and *threw clouds*. But they were no longer scared of clouds or of losing their light. Cloudy incidents were occasions for the kids to realize, again, how ineffective hurtful behavior is in meeting their real needs and to discover more respectful ways to handle their problems and *clear clouds away*.

In short, life in the valley after Zeke joins the community is much the same as life in a real classroom full of real, live rainbow kids.

The narrator concludes by wondering if the rainbow kids would have been happier if Zeke had never come into their lives. But then, the narrator notes, if Zeke had never shown up, the kids wouldn't have learned about *clearing clouds away*. The story ends with the question, "What do you think?"

▷   ▷   ▷   ▷   ▷

The Rainbow Kids Story

> **Note:** *The Rainbow Kids Story*, as it is used with students, is presented in the separate booklet in the back pocket of this book. It's also available online at http://www.ascd.org/rainbowkids. Blanks appear in both of those versions of the story to allow you to insert your students' names in the story. In addition, the story is reproduced here with children's names to give you a sense of how the story flows when it is complete.

Part I: Introduction

I would like to tell you a story about an unusual group of children, just your age, who live in a valley not far from here. If you saw these children, you might say, "What's so unusual about them? They look just like us! They have 10 fingers, and I bet if they took off their shoes, they'd have 10 toes, too! So why are they so special?"

To answer that question, you would need to spend a day or two with them. It wouldn't be long before you would notice little suns glowing inside the kids. The suns seem to be right where their hearts are—or maybe their stomachs! That's unusual enough, isn't it? But that's not all! If it began to rain while you were visiting, you would see something extraordinary. It would make you blink your eyes and shake your head and look again. And you would still see it: rainbows everywhere! For whenever it rains, the children's suns glow through the raindrops, and—zing!—rainbows appear all around them. That's why people call these children "the rainbow kids."

Of course, the kids aren't sunny all the time. Sometimes they feel sad, or disappointed, or frustrated. Have you ever felt so gloomy that it seemed like a big, heavy cloud was hanging over your head? Well, when rainbow kids feel that way, gloomy gray clouds really *do* appear, and cover their suns! Like the other day, when Jameil lost his ball. You should have seen his cloud! But later, when he found it underneath his bed, the cloud disappeared and his sun started shining brightly again.

As you can see, the rainbow kids are unusual. Yet they're like you in a lot of ways, too. They like to laugh and talk and play games and have fun together. But there's one thing they like to do most of all. They like to share their happiness and warm light with others. "Spreading sunshine"—that's what the kids call it whenever they show someone how much they care.

I know this may be hard to believe. But you don't have to take my word for it. There's a group of rainbow kids now! They're having a picnic under a tree. I see Cherie, Marco, and Theresa. And here comes Sammy, walking over to join them. Let's listen in on their conversation and find out what spreading sunshine is all about.

Scene 1: The Picnic

"Hi Cherie! Hi Marco and Theresa," said Sammy with a smile. "What are you doing?"

"We're having a picnic," answered Cherie. "Come and join us."

"Yes," said Marco. "You're just in time."

"Well, I didn't bring a lunch," said Sammy, feeling a little bit cloudy. "But I'd like to sit with you. Is there room for me?"

"Of course!" answered Theresa. "There's always room for one more. Sit here by me."

"Thanks," said Sammy, and he wiggled next to Theresa on the blanket.

"Hey, Sammy," said Cherie. "Would you like half of my sandwich? It's peanut butter and jelly."

"How about some grapes?" offered Marco. "They're the kind without seeds."

"Here," said Theresa. "If you take one of my cookies, you'll have a whole lunch!" And she put a cookie in Sammy's lap.

"Wow," laughed Sammy. "A minute ago I had nothing to eat. And now, thanks to you, I've got a great lunch! You sure have brightened my day." As Sammy spoke, his sun began to shine.

"You've made us sunnier too," said Theresa. "It feels so wonderful to share." They all nodded and smiled, and their suns grew bigger and brighter than before.

No wonder the kids liked spreading sunshine so much. The more they cared about others, the brighter their suns glowed, and the happier they felt.

Scene 2: The Marble Spill

I see some other rainbow kids! Raymond is walking across the grass toward the playground. And Katrina is heading his way. Let's listen in on their conversation.

"Hi, Raymond," said Katrina with a sunny smile. "Where are you going?"

"I'm going to play marbles with Andre," answered Raymond. He held up a bulging drawstring bag.

"That sounds like fun," said Katrina. "I've never played marbles before."

"You can join our game," said Raymond. "I'll teach you how to play."

"Great!" beamed Katrina. "It sure is nice of you to invite me." As she spoke, her sun grew brighter.

"Hey, look!" said Raymond. "There's Andre now. Let's run!"

But just as Raymond picked up speed, he tripped over his shoelace and fell down, hard. The bag flew from his hand and the marbles scattered, disappearing into the long grass.

"Raymond!" exclaimed Katrina. "Are you all right?"

"I think so," said Raymond. He brushed himself off and looked around. "Oh, no! My marbles are gone!" As he spoke, a little cloud floated in front of him.

"Don't worry," said Katrina. "I'll help you find them."

"Thanks, Katrina. I feel sunnier already." The two friends got on their hands and knees and started searching. Just then Andre arrived. When he heard what had happened he said, "Let me help!"

"Great!" said Raymond. "We'll find all the marbles in no time if we work together."

The three children laughed and talked as they searched the grass. In a jiffy, the marbles were all back in the bag. Raymond gave Katrina and Andre a thank-you hug, which made their suns shine even brighter. That was another wonderful thing about spreading sunshine: Whenever the kids were nice to someone, that person was often nice in return. You could say that whenever the kids spread sunshine to others, they ended up getting it back.

Scene 3: The Surprise Party

I see another group of rainbow kids. They're at a picnic table, working on something. Let's find out what they're doing!

Let's see, Rachel and Evan are painting yellow and red letters on a big banner. I wonder what it's going to say? Charles is busy with a box of crayons and a card. Mandy is folding colored paper into animal shapes and Chantae is making a paper chain. Look! Here comes James, walking over to join them.

"Hi, kids!" said James. "What's up?"

"We're getting ready for a surprise party," said Rachel.

"Yes," explained Evan. "Three of the rainbow kids are having birthdays this month. Look at our banner! It says "Happy Birthday Lizzy, Jameil, and Erin.""

"I'm making the birthday card!" said Charles.

"And I'm making the presents!" added Mandy.

"May I help?" asked James. "I want to spread sunshine to the birthday kids, too."

"You can help me," said Chantae.

"Great!" exclaimed James. "I love making paper chains! Do you have another stapler?"

"No," said Chantae. "But we can take turns using mine."

"Thanks," said James. He sat down next to Chantae and made a loop with a paper strip. But just as James reached for the stapler, CRASH! His elbow knocked over the can of red paint.

"Oops!" exclaimed James. Everyone snatched up projects as the paint spread quickly across the table. James got some paper towels and began mopping up the mess. Chantae ran off to get a sponge and a bucket of water.

"Oh, no!" cried Charles. "A blob of paint splashed on my card!" As he spoke, a little gray cloud appeared, and floated right in front of his sun.

"I'm sorry," said James. "It was an accident. Is there any way to fix it?"

"You could start over," suggested Mandy.

"Or maybe you could make the red blob part of the picture!" said Evan.

"I know!" said Charles, brightening up. "I can turn the blob into a red balloon."

"Great idea!" said Rachel. "It will match the balloons on our banner."

"May I use some of your yellow paint, too?" asked Charles. "I'll make a whole bunch of balloons on the card."

"Sure," said Evan. "I'll put the paint in the middle of the table so you can reach it better."

The rainbow kids got back to work.

Soon Mandy finished her project. "How do you like them?" she asked, holding up the paper animals. Mandy was holding a tall giraffe and a small frog; also a yellow lion and a brown bear. There was even a pink elephant!

"They're really great!" said Rachel.

"The birthday kids are sure going to shine when we surprise them!" said Charles.

"Yes," beamed Chantae. "And *we'll* shine, too! Hey, look! It's happening already!" Sure enough, their suns were growing brighter even as they were getting ready for the party.

Scene 4: A Sad Story and a Bright Idea

As you can tell, the rainbow kids were a happy bunch, and their lives were filled with sunshine. But one day they heard a story that really bothered them. They found out that there was a kid named Zeke who lived all by himself in a cave. The cave was dark and gloomy, and it was tucked away somewhere in the foothills near their valley. It was said that Zeke hardly ever came out of his cave.

"Poor Zeke!" the rainbow kids said. "He must not have anyone to talk to! He must not have anyone to play with!" And then they all had the same terrible thought: What if he doesn't have any sunshine? This was a very shocking idea. Their own suns seemed to shrink a little, just thinking about it!

It didn't seem fair that Zeke should be in a dark place, when the rainbow kids had so much sunshine in their lives. And one fine day, two of the rainbow kids, Audrey and Jasper, decided to do something about it. Let's find out how the adventure began.

"You know," said Audrey, as she walked along with her friend, "everything is so bright and sunny for us. I wish it could be that way for everyone."

"You're thinking about Zeke again, aren't you?" asked Jasper.

"Yes. I wish there were some way we could spread our sunshine to him."

Jasper nodded. "But how can we, if he never comes into the valley?"

"We could take our sunshine to him!" Audrey exclaimed.

"You mean, we could go find Zeke in his cave?" Jasper asked.

"Yes!" said Audrey.

"But what if Zeke likes living alone?" said Jasper. "What if he doesn't want any friends?"

"How would Zeke know if he wanted a friend if he's never had one before?" said Audrey.

"I suppose you're right," agreed Jasper. "It can't hurt to try."

"Great! Then you'll come with me?" asked Audrey.

"Sure," replied Jasper. "But how will we figure out where Zeke lives?"

"We'll just peek into every cave until we find him!" answered Audrey.

So it was decided. When Audrey and Jasper told the other kids about their plan, everyone thought it was the brightest idea they had ever heard.

The night before they left, Audrey and Jasper filled their backpacks with food, water, toothbrushes, sleeping bags, flashlights, and their favorite stuffed animals. The next morning they got up bright and early. As they set out on their journey, all the kids followed them to the edge of the valley, spreading their sunshine along the way.

"With all this sunshine," giggled Audrey, "who needs flashlights?" The two friends waved goodbye to the rest of the rainbow kids and headed out of the valley.

They climbed up, up, up into the foothills. They hiked throughout the long, warm day, stopping only to eat and drink a bit of water. Whenever they spied a cave, they peeked in. Once, they heard a noise and thought it might be Zeke. But it was only a chipmunk, scurrying across a log.

At long last the sun dropped behind the hills, and the moon and stars began twinkling. "Let's stop here for the night," Jasper said. "We can look for Zeke first thing tomorrow."

"Good idea," said Audrey. "Here's a soft, grassy place to sleep."

They unrolled their sleeping bags, curled up inside, and fell fast asleep. The glow from their suns filled the sleeping bags with a soft light that kept them safe and warm.

Now, it just so happened that Audrey and Jasper had set up their camp near the entrance to Zeke's cave. The kids hadn't noticed the cave because it was hidden behind a big bush. They didn't know how close they were to the very person they were looking for!

Zeke, of course, wasn't looking for anybody. He had been asleep, dreaming about earthworms, when the kids arrived. Their voices woke him up with a start.

"Huh?" Zeke mumbled. He didn't like being awakened from his favorite dream! But then he heard the kids' voices. "What's that?" he wondered. Zeke had never heard such a strange sound before and was very curious about it. Slowly he inched his way closer and closer to the opening of the cave. When he reached the big bush, he peeked through its branches. By this time the two kids were fast asleep.

"Huh," thought Zeke, "I wonder what they are." He studied the two kids carefully. "They look kind of like me!" he thought. But he wondered about that strange light glowing inside their covers. What could it be? Zeke looked down at himself. There was no light shining around him. Instead, he was covered with clouds. It had been that way for as long as he could remember.

Zeke stood there for a while watching the children sleep. The idea that there were other children in the world surprised him. What could it mean? He spent the rest of the night tossing and turning in his cave. He tried counting bats, but he just couldn't get to sleep.

When morning came, the kids awoke refreshed and ready to go. As they rolled up their sleeping bags, it began to sprinkle. "Oh, good," smiled

Jasper. "I bet if we look down into the valley we can see the kids' rainbows!"

Audrey searched for signs of the kids. "There they are!" she said. The gray mist hid the kids, but she could see little rainbow lights bouncing up and down as the kids ran and played together. They looked like a string of glittering jewels on a colorful necklace.

"Come on, we have to find Zeke," said Jasper. They put on their backpacks and walked down one side of the hill and up the other.

Inside the cave, Zeke was still counting. He had run out of bats and was now counting beetles. "1,256 . . . 1,257. . ." he said. Then he heard the kids' voices. "Now what happened?" Zeke wondered, scratching his head. "Oh, probably nothing, just like always." In a way, Zeke wanted it to be nothing. After all, he had lived alone for a long time. But for some reason, he just couldn't stop thinking about what he had seen and heard the night before. Finally he decided to look outside.

Once again he inched his way closer and closer to the opening of the cave. Once again he peeked through the branches of the bush. But he couldn't see anything.

Zeke almost never went out of his cave, especially in the daytime. His eyes weren't used to bright light. But it was a gray, drizzly day, and he was very curious. He took a quick step outside to have a look around.

He looked left and right. He looked up and down. But he didn't see anyone. "Nothing," he mumbled. "Nothing, nothing. I knew it."

But as Zeke turned to go back inside, a patch of tiny rainbows dancing far below in the valley suddenly caught his eye.

"Oooh! That IS something," Zeke admitted. After thinking it over, he decided to go down into the valley and find out what those rainbows were all about.

Part II
Scene 5: Zeke Meets the Rainbow Kids

Luis was the first rainbow kid to meet Zeke. He was sitting under his favorite tree, eating a snack, when he saw a sweaty, tired-looking kid coming down from the foothills. "Hi!" Luis called in his sunniest voice. "Welcome to our valley! You look like you've been walking awhile. Would you like a bite to eat?" He held up an apple.

Zeke stopped in his tracks when he heard Luis's voice. "Huh? Another one of those kids," he thought. Then he saw the apple. "Mmm. Food. I'm hungry!"

In the next instant, Zeke raced over to Luis, jumped high in the air, and crashed down on him. As Luis gave a startled cry, Zeke snatched the apple, scrambled to his feet, and dashed away.

Poor Luis didn't know what had hit him! His shoulder ached where Zeke had jumped on him. His hand was scratched where Zeke had grabbed the apple. But worst of all, Luis's feelings were hurt. Upset and confused, Luis began to cry. A cloud appeared and floated heavily in front of him.

Meanwhile, Hannah, another rainbow kid, was walking in the woods nearby. When she heard Luis's cry, she rushed to his side. "Luis! Are you all right? What happened?" she asked.

"I offered an apple to a new kid. Then he pushed me over, grabbed the apple, and ran! And now I feel really cloudy," said Luis.

"Of course you do!" said Hannah as she put her arm around him. "I'm sorry you're hurt. Would you like me to get you another apple?"

"Thanks," said Luis. "I don't really care about the apple. I'm feeling cloudy because of that kid. I wonder why he pushed me and grabbed the apple?"

"I don't know," said Hannah. "Maybe he didn't understand that you were trying to give it to him."

"Yeah, maybe," replied Luis.

"Why don't we spread sunshine to him? Then he'll know you were trying to be his friend."

"Okay," agreed Luis. "But we'll have to find him first."

"Which way did he go?" Hannah asked. She helped Luis to his feet.

"That way," Luis answered, pointing in the direction of the playground. "Let's go." They followed the path that Zeke had taken.

Soon they came to a drinking fountain. And there was Erin, sitting on the ground, looking cloudy. Zeke had shoved her out of the way so he could get a drink.

"We've got to make friends with that kid before he makes everyone cloudy!" said Hannah. They helped Erin to her feet, and all three of them continued down the path.

By that time, Zeke had reached the playground where the rest of the kids were. He stood at the edge of the field and watched as they happily jumped rope and played games with balls and other toys.

"Huh," Zeke thought. "Why do they smile so much? They look happy. I want to get happy like them."

Zeke thought about the balls and the jump ropes and the other toys the kids were playing with. "Toys make them happy!" he decided. "I'll take the toys. Then I can get happy, too!"

In a flash, Zeke swooped down on the rainbow kids and grabbed as many toys as he could. He roughly pushed aside anyone who got in his way. With each shove came more and more clouds. Soon, the whole playground was covered with huge, dark storm clouds.

By the time Hannah, Luis, and Erin got to the playground, Zeke was running off, his arms loaded with toys. "Come back!" shouted Hannah. "Why did you push us down? Where are you going with our toys? Why won't you be our friend?"

But as soon as Zeke heard Hannah's voice, he doubled his speed. He ran up, up, up into the foothills. He didn't stop until he reached his cave.

"There," said Zeke, dumping the toys into a corner. "Now I can get happy too." He sat down and waited for the toys to make him happy. But nothing happened.

"Huh," Zeke grunted. He kicked the toys all over the cave. "They're good for nothing. Nothing, nothing. Just like everything else." Then he curled up under his dark cloud and fell fast asleep.

That was the day that everything changed for the rainbow kids. Even after Zeke left, the clouds stayed in the valley. Have you ever felt so gloomy that it seemed like nothing could make things better? That's how it was for the rainbow kids. With all those clouds around, they couldn't seem to find their suns. And once they lost touch with their light, their happy feelings disappeared too. The kids became scared and confused. They were so busy worrying about themselves that they forgot to care about each other.

They started acting differently, too. When they saw something they wanted, they grabbed it. If someone got in their way, they pushed. Instead of making friends, they began losing friends. Each time someone's feelings were hurt, the clouds surrounding the kids grew bigger and darker than ever. Before long, the whole valley was hidden under a thick cloud cover. Worst of all, when it rained, there were no rainbows. It takes sunshine to make a rainbow, and the kids' suns were nowhere in sight.

Scene 6: The Dazzling Duo Meets Zeke

Meanwhile, Audrey and Jasper were still searching the foothills for Zeke. Although they had found many caves, they hadn't found Zeke. They began to wonder if he had moved, or if there really *was* a Zeke! They missed their home and their rainbow friends. Finally they decided to give up the search. They headed through the foothills and back toward their valley. As they reached the top of the last hill, it began to rain.

"Oh, good!" exclaimed Audrey. "Now the kids' rainbows will show us the way home." She looked eagerly down into the valley. But to her surprise, there were no rainbows shining below.

"That's strange," Jasper said, with a puzzled look. "I wonder where the kids are?"

"Maybe it's not raining in the valley," said Audrey.

"It looks like it is, though," said Jasper. "Well, it's almost dark. Why don't we camp here for the night?"

"Okay, but let's find someplace dry," said Audrey. She began to look for a place that would shelter them from the rain. Suddenly she saw something. "Hey, Jasper! Over here, behind this big bush. It's a cave! We must have missed it the first time."

"Great! See if it's empty," Jasper said.

Audrey peeked into the cave and called softly, "Anybody home?" When no one answered, she shouted back to Jasper, "It's just another empty cave. Come on in. It's nice and dry in here."

Can you guess what happened next? Audrey and Jasper walked right into Zeke's cave! Of course, they didn't know it because they couldn't see him sitting quietly in a cloudy corner, all the way in the back.

Zeke recognized them at once. "It's those smiling kids again," he thought. "They look so happy. And they don't even have toys. They must have a secret way to get happy."

Zeke watched from his corner until Audrey and Jasper fell asleep. Then he decided to creep closer. When he got to the front of the cave, the light from the kids' suns reached Zeke's cold skin. "Mmm, that feels good," thought Zeke, as he began to warm up. "It must be the light that makes the kids happy. If I take some light, I'll be happy, too."

Zeke reached down to scoop up the light, but it slipped right through his fingers. "Huh," he thought. "The light stays with the kids. I guess I need the whole kid!" Slowly Zeke dragged Jasper, sleeping bag and all, into his cloudy corner. Soon his corner was light and warm.

Jasper didn't know that he was spreading sunshine in his sleep! Zeke didn't know it, either. He just knew that he liked the warmth and light. "I got some happy!" he thought as he fell asleep.

In the morning, Jasper was the first to wake up. He gave a big yawn and tried to stretch. But he couldn't move. He felt like a teddy bear, being held by a big baby! For Zeke had fallen asleep with his arm around Jasper's sleeping bag.

Startled, Jasper said, "Is that you, Audrey?"

"What?" mumbled Audrey from the front of the cave. She opened her eyes and looked around. "Jasper, where are you?"

"I'm back here, in the corner," whispered Jasper.

"What are you doing there?" Audrey whispered back.

"I think I'm being a teddy bear!" said Jasper, laughing quietly. "And I found who we're looking for!"

"You found Zeke?"

"Actually, he found me," Jasper answered.

"Horray!" Audrey shouted. "We found him!"

Audrey's shout woke Zeke up. Zeke yelled "Huh?" and jumped as if he had been stung by a bee.

"Wait, Audrey!" Jasper said quickly. "Don't come too close yet. Zeke seems scared. Let me make friends with him first."

Then Jasper spoke to Zeke in his warmest, friendliest voice. He told Zeke how long he had been looking for him, how happy he was to meet him, and how much he wanted to be his friend.

Zeke just backed further into his corner and looked at Jasper suspiciously. The clouds got thicker and thicker in the cave.

"Are you friends yet?" Audrey asked.

"No," replied Jasper. "I don't think Zeke understands a word I've said. He doesn't look like he trusts me. Now what should we do?"

"If we can't *tell* him we want to be his friend, we'll have to *show* him," said Audrey. "I bet he'll get the message if we fill his whole cave with sunshine."

"Good idea," answered Jasper. "But it's going to take more than the two of us to light up this cloudy place."

"I know!" said Audrey. "I'll go get the rainbow kids. All their sunshine will make this cave as bright as day!"

"Okay!" said Jasper, "I'll keep trying to make friends with Zeke."

"Great. 'Bye!" Audrey called out as she left the cave. "I'll be back as soon as I can!" And she raced down the hill in search of the rainbow kids.

**Part III
Scene 7: The Hide and Seek Game**

By the time Audrey reached the valley, she was completely out of breath. She slowed her step and noticed how strange everything felt. The air was thick and gray, and although it was sprinkling, there wasn't a rainbow in sight.

"Something must be wrong!" thought Audrey. "The valley has never felt like this before."

She continued walking to the park where the kids usually played. "I wonder where they could be," she said as she passed the empty swings. Then Audrey heard voices from the far end of the field. There were the kids, playing hide and seek. From where she stood, she could see Kristin, Edgar, and Silvia dashing toward the trees. Lizzy was crawling under a bush. And Stephan and Jameil were piling leaves on top of each other.

Just then Julie, who was "it," finished counting. "80 . . . 90 . . . 100! Here I come, ready or not!" Julie uncovered her eyes, and after a quick look around, found Dennis crouched beneath the picnic table.

"I see you, Dennis!" Julie shouted. "You're out!"

"Cheater!" Dennis yelled. "You peeked! There's no way you could find me that fast!" As Dennis spoke, a dark cloud zoomed directly from him to Julie.

"I did not peek!" Julie yelled back. "Anyone could find you in that dumb hiding place!" With Julie's angry words, the same cloud zoomed straight back at Dennis—only it was bigger than before.

"My hiding place was not dumb!" cried Dennis. "I'm not playing with a bunch of cheaters! I quit!" The cloud, bigger than ever, flung itself at Julie.

"We don't want you in our game anyway. Who wants to play with a sore loser like you!" Julie yelled.

Like a ping-pong ball, the cloud zipped back and forth with each angry word. More clouds rushed in as the two kids continued to fight. Soon Julie and Dennis were trapped in a huge storm.

Audrey was shocked. "What has happened while I've been gone?" she thought. "Julie and Dennis are throwing clouds at each other! They're making an awful storm! Someone's got to stop them!"

But the other kids were still hiding, too scared to come out. They had been trapped in a lot of ugly storms lately, and they weren't about to walk into the middle of this one.

Audrey knew she had to do something. She stepped between Julie and Dennis and, with arms outstretched, shouted, "Stop! Both of you! Can't you see, you're hurting yourselves!"

When the other kids heard Audrey's voice, their heads popped out from their hiding places. "It's Audrey!" Kristin called to the others. "She's back!"

"Oh, no!" said Edgar. "We've got to warn her about storms. Audrey! Quick, get out of the way! The clouds will hurt you!"

But it was too late. All the clouds that had gathered in the angry storm between Dennis and Julie were hurtling straight to Audrey. The first dark cloud crashed into her hand and moved up her arm. Without thinking, Audrey raised her other hand and brushed the cloud off. The next cloud zoomed toward her chest, but Audrey took a step aside and let it tumble past. And then, the biggest, blackest cloud flew directly at Audrey's face. She calmly took a breath of air, and with one big puff, blew it away.

"That's amazing!" exclaimed Silvia. "She's in the middle of a storm, and she's still sunny and bright!" Sure enough, the rest of the clouds glided right past Audrey as if she weren't there. Instead, they settled around Dennis and Julie, who were sitting on the ground crying.

"Audrey! How did you stay sunny?" shouted Lizzy crawling out of her hiding place.

"I just stepped out of the way," Audrey answered. "Those clouds have nothing to do with me."

"But that never happens to me," said Stephan. "Whenever clouds are thrown my way, they always stick!"

"Yes," said the rest of the kids. "Why do clouds always stick to us?"

"Maybe it's because we're already cloudy," Jameil said. "You know how angry clouds like to stick together."

"That's true!" said Lizzy. "Look at Audrey. She's so sunny, the clouds have nothing to stick to!"

"Well, that's fine for Audrey," said Edgar. "But what about the rest of us? We're already cloudy, so the clouds will keep on sticking to us!"

"Why don't you clear the clouds away?" Audrey suggested.

"Clear them away?" asked the kids in surprise. "How?"

"I have an idea," said Audrey. She walked over to Dennis and helped him up. "Dennis, how did you feel when Julie found you hiding?"

"Mad!" said Dennis. "I hate getting caught first."

"Do you remember what you said when you got caught?" asked Audrey.

"I think I called Julie a cheater," said Dennis, looking uncomfortable.

"Did you notice? That's when the storm began," said Audrey.

Julie burst out, "Anyway, Dennis, I *didn't* peek! I could see your bright red shirt from a mile away!"

"Yes," said Audrey. "But instead of telling Dennis that, you called his hiding place 'dumb.' That sent the angry cloud right back at Dennis."

"Yeah, Julie!" Dennis grumbled. "When you called my hiding place 'dumb,' it felt like you were calling *me* dumb."

Now Julie looked uncomfortable. She thought for a moment. "I'm sorry about what I said, Dennis. I was mad because you said I cheated."

"Well, I guess I shouldn't have called you a cheater," admitted Dennis. "I just didn't see how you could find me so fast. I forgot about my shirt."

Then Julie had an idea. "Hey, why don't you borrow my brown sweat-shirt? Put it on, and we'll start over again!" She pulled her sweatshirt off and handed it to Dennis.

"Thanks, Julie!" Dennis smiled. "I promise not to call you a cheater if you find me this time."

"Okay, everybody!" Julie shouted to the rest of the kids. "We're starting the game over!"

"Wait!" shouted Jameil, pointing at Dennis and Julie. "Look what's hap-pening!" All the kids stared. Two bright sunbeams were bursting through the clouds that had been hanging gloomily around Julie and Dennis.

"Wow!" exclaimed the kids. "Their clouds are clearing away! Hooray for Audrey!"

"How did you do it?" asked Silvia in amazement.

"I didn't do it," Audrey replied. "The clouds began clearing as soon as Dennis and Julie started caring about each other!"

"You mean, it's that easy?" Kristin asked.

"Sure!" said Audrey with a smile. "If hurtful words bring clouds, then caring words clear them away!"

"What a relief!" said Dennis. "I thought I was stuck with these clouds forever!"

"Me, too," said Julie. "Thanks, Audrey. It's a good thing you came back."

"Where's Jasper?" asked Stephan.

"Oh, no!" exclaimed Audrey. "I almost forgot! Jasper is waiting for us in Zeke's cave."

"Zeke's cave?" asked the kids. "You mean you found Zeke?"

"Well, actually Zeke found us. You see, it all began last night when it started to rain."

Then Audrey told the kids the whole story: how they had camped in Zeke's cave, how Zeke had pulled Jasper into his cloudy corner, how surprised Jasper was in the morning to find Zeke there, and how hard it was to make friends with Zeke because he couldn't talk.

"And that's why we need everyone's help," Audrey finished. "If we fill Zeke's cave with sunshine and light, we know he'll want to be friends."

The kids sadly shook their heads. "We'd like to help," said Rachel, "but I'm afraid we can't."

"You see," explained Andre, "we don't have any sunshine to spread. All our clouds drove the sunshine away."

"What? No sunshine to spread?" Audrey smiled at the kids. "That's not true. Your suns are still shining. You just need to clear the clouds so you can see them again. Look at what happened to Julie and Dennis!"

The kids looked at each other sadly. Then Marco said, "But our suns have been gone for such a long time."

"If you don't believe me, I'll just have to show you," said Audrey. "Is there anyone who will help Jasper and me?" She looked at all their faces.

Erin spoke up first. "I want to help. I'll come."

"We'll come, too," added Charles and Kristin.

Now every kid was looking at Audrey. "We'll all come. Show us the way."

"It's just up this path. Follow me!" Once again, Audrey headed up into the foothills. The kids were right behind her. It wasn't long before they all arrived at Zeke's cave.

Scene 8: The Grand Finale

"What should we do now?" asked Lizzy.

"We don't want to scare Zeke," said Audrey. "So, we'll have to be very quiet. When we get inside, let's hold hands and sit in a circle."

Inside the cave, Jasper heard their voices and called out, "Audrey? Is that you? Did you bring the kids?"

"Yes!" whispered Audrey. "We're coming in!" Joining hands, the kids tiptoed into the cave. Even though it was dark, they managed to form a circle.

"You're here at last!" whispered Jasper. "I still haven't been able to get Zeke to trust me." Zeke looked at the kids suspiciously. Then Jasper added, "Your suns are such a welcome sight."

"Our suns?" exclaimed the kids, looking around. Sure enough, there, in the darkness of the cave, the kids could see little lights glowing deep inside them. Their happy walk in the foothills together, and their hopes for helping Audrey and Jasper, had started clearing away the clouds they had carried for so long.

"Hooray! It worked!" Audrey beamed when she saw their suns. The kids' faces broke into grins, which made their lights shine even brighter.

Now the cave filled with light, and the clouds slowly melted. As the warmth washed over Zeke, he started to relax. All of a sudden, he had a new thought. "I don't need to *take* happy. These smiling kids are *giving* me happy!" Then something very unusual happened to Zeke. The corners of his mouth turned up. It was the beginning of Zeke's very first smile.

Jasper walked over to Zeke and gently placed his arm around him. "I think Zeke likes having friends now," said Jasper.

But with all the new light in the cave, the kids were able to see Zeke clearly for the first time. Evan was the first kid to recognize Zeke. "Uh-oh!" he whispered. "Isn't that the same kid who threw the clouds at us?"

"Yes!" gasped Mandy. "And look over there in the corner—aren't those our toys?"

The kids' lights began to fade when they realized who Zeke was.

"Well, he's not throwing clouds now," Stephan said. "And I sure don't remember him smiling like that before!"

All the kids stared at Zeke. Zeke didn't even notice, he was so happy and warm.

"Look!" cried Theresa pointing at Zeke. "He's got a sun!" And there, shining in the center of Zeke's chest, was a tiny glowing light.

"Of course he's got a sun," said Audrey. "Everyone's got a sun."

"I bet he never felt his sun before," Edgar remarked.

"Yeah," agreed Silvia. "He was so covered with clouds, he probably didn't even know he had a sun."

"Just like us, before Audrey came back," added Jameil. The rest of the kids nodded as they realized how like Zeke they were. Their suns started shining brightly again.

"Hey! I've got an idea," said Cherie. "Why don't we invite Zeke to come back to our valley? Then he won't have to stay in this dark place anymore."

"Yes, yes, let's do it!" said all the others.

Jasper held his hand out to Zeke. "We're going home now, Zeke. Would you like to come with us?"

Zeke's smile got bigger as he placed his hand in Jasper's.

"I guess that answers our question!" said Audrey. "Let's go home!"

Just as the kids left the cave, a soft rain began to fall. One by one, a dazzling line of rainbows went marching down the hill. The most special rainbow of them all was the little one that circled the smiling kid who was holding hands with Jasper.

Epilogue

And that's how Zeke ended up living in the valley. It wasn't too long before he learned to talk, and to ask for what he wanted instead of grabbing. Zeke even learned how to spread sunshine! And, maybe because he had lived for so long in a dark, cloudy cave, Zeke enjoyed spreading sunshine most of all. He loved the warm feelings that come when you care about others.

The kids had learned something from Zeke, too. They realized that, no matter what the weather, their suns were always shining inside them. They were no longer scared of clouds or of losing their light. Of course, every once in awhile, they would still get angry and throw clouds. But then they would remember that throwing clouds makes things worse for everyone, and they would get busy clearing the clouds away.

Sometimes I wonder if the rainbow kids would have been happier if Zeke had never entered their lives. But maybe it was better for everybody that he did. It was certainly better for Zeke, because he found his sun and didn't have to live in a dark place anymore. And maybe it was better for the kids, too, because they learned more about clouds and how to clear them away. After all, dealing with clouds is a part of real life.

What do you think?

The End

4

Nuts and Bolts of Presenting the Program

Now that you are acquainted with the story of the rainbow kids and the concepts it's designed to teach, you are ready to present the program to children. This chapter walks you through the implementation process: making preparations, personalizing the story, creating the symbols, and establishing a schedule. After that, you'll get suggestions about telling the story to students and delivering the follow-up lessons and activities. All of these steps are summarized on the Implementation Checklist, Figure 4.1 (p. 68). The chapter ends with ideas about involving parents and making the program your own.

Cast the Characters

To help students identify with the characters in the story, give the rainbow kids in the story the names of the students in your class. Numbered blanks appear in the story (see booklet or online) whenever a child's name is needed; assigning each student's name a number simplifies the process.

The story is divided into eight scenes, with several children appearing in each scene. To help cast your students into roles, the scenes and a brief

4.1
IMPLEMENTATION CHECKLIST

Get Ready

_____ 1. Personalize the story. Put the names of your students in *The Rainbow Kids Story* (either using the booklet in the back of the book or online at http://www.ascd.org/rainbowkids). Use the information in Figure 4.2, Casting Worksheet, to help you assign students to roles. Once each student has a number, fill in the story's blanks with students' names. Additional information about personalizing the story can be found in "Cast the Characters" at the beginning of Chapter 4.

_____ 2. Make the symbols. The suns, clouds, and rainbows can be made out of construction paper or flannel. For complete instructions for making the symbols, see Appendix A. You may wish to make extra symbols to decorate the charts that are used in the lessons.

_____ 3. Establish a schedule. Rehearse. Schedule ten 20-minute periods on consecutive days to present the story and follow-up lessons (see Figure 4.3 for a sample schedule). Practice reading the story aloud while holding up the appropriate symbols.

Present the Program

_____ 4. Read *The Rainbow Kids Story* to your class. Reading the story will take about three days of 20-minute class periods. You can use your regular story time.

_____ 5. Present the seven lessons found in Part II.

Live the Lessons

Coach and support children as they learn to apply the concepts and skills to new situations.

_____ 6. *Spreading Sunshine*. Point out thoughtful, caring behavior by saying, "That's *spreading sunshine*." Remind children to *spread sunshine* whenever it is appropriate—when a guest visits, on field trips, during a trip to the library. Point out *sunny* themes in stories or songs.

_____ 7. *Clouds*. When children report their upsets, listen and acknowledge their feelings. Label hurtful behavior, "That's a *cloud*." Help children become aware of their own hurtful behavior by pointing out the negative effects.

_____ 8. *Clear Clouds Away*. When children come to you with problems, ask, "What could you do to *clear the cloud away*?" Coach and support children as they learn to solve their problems using the 4-step process (see How to Help Children Clear Clouds Away, Appendix D). As children become skillful, encourage them to solve problems on their own.

description of each role are listed in the Casting Worksheet, Figure 4.2. As you consider which roles to assign your students, remember that the rainbow kids live in a community where children openly care about everyone. Here's a chance to show how your students might behave under these conditions. Place your students in the most positive social groupings. Put boys and girls together. Make sure each group is ethnically mixed. Break up cliques and spread out positive leaders. Place less popular children in favorable positions. For example, a child who is often socially left out in the classroom might be given the role of kid 5, who is invited to join a picnic. An aggressive child might be cast as kid 7, who is shown helping a friend. All roles are suitable for either boys or girls. Don't forget to adjust the pronouns in the story to match the gender of the student in each role.

The casting of kids 15 and 16 needs special consideration because these two characters play a central role in the development of the story. Choose students who have qualities similar to those of the characters in the story. Kids 15 and 16 are both gentle and loving children, with a genuine concern for the welfare of others. Kid 15 also has good ideas and is a natural leader. It is kid 15 who teaches the others to *clear clouds away* and who leads the group back to Zeke's cave at the end of the story. Select a girl and a boy for these roles so that both genders identify with the lead characters.

The story is written for 24 students. If your class is larger than 24, create another *spreading sunshine* vignette and add it to the story after Scene 3. If you have fewer than 24 students, double up on some of the parts or omit one of the *spreading sunshine* scenes in Part I. Also, feel free to modify the story to make it more relevant and appealing to your class. For example, if your students have never played with marbles, change the marbles in Scene 2 to trading cards or some other plaything your

FIGURE 4.2
CASTING WORKSHEET

This worksheet provides a brief description of the 24 rainbow kid characters and their respective scenes. To personalize the story, fill in the blanks with the names of your students. All roles are suitable for boys or girls. Change the pronoun in the story to match the gender of the child assigned. For more information about placing your students in the story, see the section "Cast the Characters" at the beginning of Chapter 4.

Part I

Introduction
1._____ loses his ball and finds it

Scene 1: The Picnic
2._____, 3._____ and 4._____ eat a picnic lunch; 5._____ joins and is given food by the group

Scene 2: The Marble Spill
6._____ spills his marbles on the way to the playground;
7._____ is invited to play and helps pick up marbles; 8._____ arrives later and also helps

Scene 3: The Surprise Party
9._____ and 10._____ paint a banner; 11._____ makes a card that is later splashed with paint; 12._____ makes gifts; 13._____ makes a paper chain; 14._____ joins the group, helps make the paper chain, and accidentally spills paint

Additional Scene (optional)
If you have more than 24 students, write another *spreading sunshine* scene and add it here.

Scene 4: A Sad Story and a Bright Idea
15._____ and 16._____ leave the valley in search of Zeke

Part II

Scene 5: Zeke Meets the Rainbow Kids
17._____ offers Zeke an apple and gets a cloud in return; 18._____ comforts 16._____ and they go off in search of Zeke; 19._____ is pushed at the water fountain

---

FIGURE 4.2
CASTING WORKSHEET (CONTINUED)

Scene 6: The Dazzling Duo Meet Zeke
No new characters

Part III

In addition to introducing kids 20–24, the last two scenes have speaking parts for several other children. These parts are arbitrarily assigned here to students who have smaller parts earlier in the story.

Scene 7: The Hide and Seek Game
20._____, 21._____, 22._____, 23._____, 24._____, and 1._____ play hide and seek;
9._____, 8._____, 3._____, 19._____ and 11._____ join the conversation about clouds and helping light Zeke's cave

Scene 8: The Grand Finale
24._____, 10._____, 12._____, 23._____, 4._____, 21._____, 22._____, 1._____, and 2._____ discover their suns and Zeke's in the cave

---

children have experienced. If valleys and hills are not familiar to your students, change the setting of the story to match the geography of your area. Look for other details, too, that may need adjusting to match your students' experience. One teacher left out the reference to "favorite stuffed animals" in Scene 4 because her 2nd graders might think that was too babyish.

In addition to the 24 numbered roles, there are three characters in the story who model aggressive behavior and for that reason are not given names of the students in your class. These characters have already been assigned names. Zeke is the socially unskillful child who *throws clouds* at the rainbow kids, and Dennis and Julie fight during the hide-and-seek game in Scene 7. If you happen to have a Zeke, Dennis, or Julie in your class, choose other names for those three characters.

Make the Weather Symbols

Young children learn best from concrete objects. It is therefore important to show children the appropriate weather symbol whenever a character's emotions change. A ❖ appears in the text of the story each time a symbol is needed, and a picture cue is shown in the margin to indicate which symbol to display. So, for example, a bigger sun is shown after the kids *spread sunshine.* A cloud is held in front of the sun after a hurtful incident of *cloud throwing.* The cloud is removed when hurt feelings are reconciled or *cleared away.* In this way, children see how their positive and negative actions result in visible changes in their emotions and the emotions of those around them.

The suns and clouds come in three different sizes and can be made with construction paper or flannel. A few rainbows are also needed to show what happens when the *sunny* kids play in the rain. You may wish to make extra suns and clouds to use on the charts in the follow-up lessons. For complete instructions on preparing these materials, see Appendix A: Symbols (p. 145).

Establish a Schedule

It takes approximately two weeks, or ten 20-minute periods, to present this program—three sessions to tell the story and seven sessions to present the follow-up lessons. The story may be presented during regular story time or in any 20-minute period. Each lesson builds upon the previous one, so it

---

FIGURE 4.3
SCHEDULE FOR PRESENTING THE RAINBOW KIDS PROGRAM

Day 1   Part I of the story
Day 2   Part II of the story
Day 3   Part III of the story, Illustrate the Story (Optional Activity)
Day 4   Lesson 1: I Feel Sunny or Cloudy
Day 5   Lesson 2: We Spread Sunshine
Day 6   Lesson 3: We Feel Cloudy
Day 7   Lesson 4: We Clear Clouds Away (Introduction)
Day 8   Lesson 5: How To Cool Off (Step 1)
Day 9   Lesson 6: How To Talk and Listen (Step 2)
Day 10   Lesson 7: How To Brainstorm and Choose (Steps 3 & 4)
  Note: Empathy Game is an optional activity that can be presented any time after Lesson 1.

---

works best to schedule the sessions over ten consecutive days. A sample schedule appears in Figure 4.3 to help you make plans.

As with any good teaching plan, be responsive to students' needs and change the schedule accordingly. Allow students to set the pace as you move through the materials. If the story becomes too long, especially for young children, simply stop at the end of a scene and resume where you left off the next day. Some Kindergarten teachers have found that they need four or even five days to finish the story. When presenting the lessons, you may decide to spend more than one day on some of the activities. For example, in Lesson 2, you and your children may enjoy observing and recording *spreading sunshine* incidents for several days before moving on to Lesson 3.

Another scheduling consideration is deciding when in the school year to present the program. Although it is tempting to use the program to establish a caring environment at the start of school, the story is more meaningful after you and your students have considerable experience living and working together. The personalities of the characters in the story rely upon students' knowledge of their classmates. The better your students know one another, the richer the story becomes. It is also easier for you to place students in the story when you know their unique personalities and the dynamics of the class.

Many teachers prefer to introduce the program after the winter holiday, when everyone returns to school refreshed but a bit disoriented. The program works to pull the class together and focus special attention upon establishing a positive, caring environment. By January, too, there may be a greater need to sharpen children's social skills. The honeymoon period is well past, and children feel comfortable being themselves, which often means frustrating situations and interpersonal conflict. What better time to teach and practice emotional and social skills than when children need them the most?

Rehearse the Story

Your expression and eye contact are important to make the story come alive. Before each day's presentation, rehearse the story a few times to familiarize yourself with the plot, the characters, and the symbols to be used so that your eyes can leave the page and make contact with your students.

Don't worry about saying every word. When two characters are engaged in dialogue, for example, you can sometimes change your voice to indicate which character is speaking and drop the "he said, she said" verbiage. It is more important to tell the story in your most engaging way than to read the story verbatim. As long as you are faithful to the basic plot, you're doing the job.

Tell the Story to Students

The Rainbow Kids Story is different from the usual read-aloud book and needs a special introduction. You might begin by telling students, "I am going to tell a make-believe story about you. In the story you are called rainbow kids and if you listen carefully, you will be able to hear your name."

Let students know that the story takes several days to tell, so many will not hear their name until the second or third day. (You may decide to tell students ahead of time who will be in the story that day to prevent disappointed groans at the end.) Also, let children know that because the story is not illustrated, they will have to rely on their own imaginations to make pictures. If you decide to have students illustrate the story (Illustrate the Story Activity is in Part II), you may tell them in advance that they will be doing their own illustrations later in the week.

It is exciting, even embarrassing, for some children when they first hear their names and visualize themselves in the story. Be prepared for giggles. The tittering usually tapers off as children get used to this special feature of the story.

Finally, with the text in your lap and the symbols within reach, "read-tell" the story in your most engaging storytelling voice. Display the appropriate symbols whenever they are indicated. Before you begin the story each day, briefly review the events read about in the previous days. Young children especially need to be reminded of the previous episode, and they love the repetition.

Present the Lessons and Activities

You may be surprised to discover that, after hearing the conclusion of *The Rainbow Kids Story*, your students will not automatically *spread sunshine* and *clear clouds away*. The subject matter is so obvious to us—everyday feelings and actions—that it's easy to assume that children will internalize the skills as soon as they are presented. In fact, social and emotional instruction is not different from the teaching of any other subject. When we teach reading, for example, we don't expect students to be able to read after hearing the letter sounds once. Instead, we systematically introduce letter sounds and give children practice decoding words. At the same time, we immerse them in a world of language and books and help them make sense of that world. We teach children to be socially and emotionally competent by introducing key concepts and skills, by surrounding them with opportunities to socialize, and by coaching them to use the skills whenever appropriate.

The lessons and activities provided in Part II are designed to do just that. Each lesson relates the story to children's personal experience, instructs them in the development of specific skills, and provides opportunities for practice. Additional suggestions at the end of each lesson can help children use the new skills in their daily social lives. These suggestions are presented under the heading "Ideas for Living the Lessons," where you will also find supplementary activities developed by other rainbow kids' teachers and lists of children's books that emphasize the themes featured in the lessons.

Introduce *Rainbow Kids* to Parents

If you fully implement the *Rainbow Kids Program*, you may discover, as I did, that children take the ideas home and try them out with their families. Shortly after that, parents may be at your door asking for an explanation. One mother reported that her daughter was "*spreading sunshine*" around the house and, although she didn't quite understand what that meant, she liked the effects and wanted to know how she could encourage the behavior. The day after I introduced How to Cool Off (Lesson 5), the mother of a quick-tempered boy told me that he had come home from school and immediately set up a "feelings place" in his room so he could "cool off." She liked the sound of this place and was eager to hear more. Still another parent sheepishly reported that during an argument she was having with her husband, her daughter advised them to stop *throwing clouds* and *clear them away* instead. "What exactly does that mean?" she asked me.

If we truly want children to internalize the social skills and emotional understandings presented in the program, it makes sense to bring parents on board so they can reinforce the ideas at home. Imagine how much quicker children will learn to solve their social problems, for example, if parents are supporting them to *clear clouds away* using the same language and processes. Teachers and parents are, after all, partners in the job of educating children. The more we talk and share, the more consistent our message to kids and the more likely they will master the skills we think are important. It has also been my experience that, when it comes to helping their children get along with one another, parents are grateful for help.

Once I learned that parents were likely to ask questions about the program, I became proactive about educating them. A week before reading the story to children I sent home a newsletter announcing that *Rainbow Kids* was coming, explaining the program's goals, and introducing the concepts and skills using rainbow kid language. (A sample letter to parents appears in Appendix F). I also invited parents to ask questions as they came up and encouraged them to visit and observe what we were doing. During parent-teacher conferences and open houses I offered an update on the program and prominently displayed rainbow kid artifacts (class books, art, posters, and charts).

Parents were always quick (and pleased) to discover their child's name on the We Spread Sunshine and We Clear Clouds Away charts. And, because the concepts are so easy to understand, parents learned a great deal by simply reading the materials on the walls. One year, the parents were so enthusiastic about *Rainbow Kids* that I offered an evening workshop to explain the program in greater detail and offered tips for helping their children *clear clouds away* at home.

Make the Program Your Own

Like other teachers, you will no doubt find wonderful new ways to reinforce the lessons in daily classroom life and extend the ideas into other areas of the curriculum. Have fun adding art projects, rainbow science experiments, and *sunny* songs. Look for ways to *spread sunshine* inside and outside the classroom. When you read aloud to the class, point out the *cloudy* feelings of the characters and how they chose to express their feelings. Did their actions result in more *clouds* or did *clouds clear away*? Coach and support children to *clear away* their real *clouds* when disagreements occur. Examine the persistent problem behaviors in your class and develop new lessons that teach children the skills they are missing. If you send me your ideas, I'll share them with others, with credit to you (a response form is provided on p. 169). I also welcome your comments, suggestions, criticisms, and questions.

Cautionary Tales

As you add your own creative touch to the *Rainbow Kids Program*, be careful that your refinements are consistent with the program's underlying principles. When the concepts are used in ways that were not intended, you undermine the program's effectiveness and run the risk of teaching something altogether different. Three examples come to mind.

One teacher who had taken the *Rainbow Kids* workshop reported that she made a rainbow crown to be worn by the child who *spread* the most *sunshine* that day. The reward of getting to wear the special crown, she concluded, further motivated her children to care about each other.

I argue that the crown reward had the opposite effect. While one child got to be sunshine queen for the day and the impression that she was

better than everybody else, the rest of the class may have been feeling disappointed, jealous, or resentful that their good deeds were not good enough. The losers might double their efforts to win the next day or they might give up because the crown reward wasn't motivating enough. But in either case, the children learn nothing about altruism and the good feelings that automatically come when they care about others. Instead, they learn that if they comply with the teacher and if they are deemed best, they will be rewarded. I suspect that when a substitute is teaching (and wearing the crown is not a possibility), the *spreading sunshine* contest is off.

I heard about another teacher who kept a tally sheet on students' desks that tracked the number of *clouds* they had *thrown*. Later the students who threw *clouds* were given consequences; the higher the incidence of *clouds*, the more severe the consequence. If children perceived those consequences as punishment, the program had little chance of success: Punished children are not likely to buy into *clearing clouds away* when the teacher routinely *throws clouds* at them. If we want students to solve their problems respectfully, we must model those same skills when we have problems with students.

Although it is beyond the scope of this book to investigate disciplinary strategies that are philosophically aligned with the *Rainbow Kids*, there are excellent books listed in the Selected Resources section (p. 159). You might also want to read Chapters 8 and 9 of *Talk It Out: Conflict Resolution in the Elementary Classroom* (Porro, 1996), which give a detailed description of how to approach student-teacher conflicts using the same problem solving steps described in the *clearing clouds away* process.

Finally, several other teachers reported that although they loved the *spreading sunshine* lesson, they skipped the lessons about *cloudy* feelings and *clearing clouds away* because they feared being overwhelmed by tattled tales once problems became a legitimate topic of conversation. It is true that children may feel more comfortable talking about problems after they've explored their *cloudy* feelings in the lessons. But if teachers are not available to work with *clouds*, I worry that children might get the message that only *sunny* feelings and caring actions are welcome in the room. The program was not designed to establish utopia or to even suggest that it's possible to achieve utopia. As pleasant as it sounds, that idealistic place doesn't exist. Instead, the program is designed to teach children that

clouds are as natural a feature of the human landscape as *suns.* When *clouds* appear in the classroom, as they often do in life, it is up to the teacher to guide and support children to make choices that create more light in their lives.

An even larger lesson may be to help children appreciate *clouds* as gifts that challenge them to grow. Think about how Zeke affected the rainbow kids. Thanks to the adversity he created, the kids confronted their fear of big *clouds*, figured out how to deal with their painful feelings effectively, and discovered they can always count on their source of light. Though Rainbow Valley was nice before Zeke's *clouds* made the scene, life no doubt became more vivid, lively, and dimensional in the post-Zeke era. Once the kids realized it was safe to experience the full spectrum of emotions, particularly the scary end, I suspect that their *suns* and *clouds* got bigger and their *rainbows* shined brighter than before.

A Last Word

The incidents related as cautionary tales are a humble reminder that what we teach is a function of who we are and what we believe, not of what is written in the curriculum. Running students through this or any other social skills program is no guarantee that they will become socially competent or emotionally intelligent. Changing the way children handle their feelings and relate to one another requires nothing short of transforming ourselves, the adults responsible for modeling the skills that establish a caring classroom community. Perhaps this book will help light the way for teachers as well as children.

▷　▷　▷　▷　▷

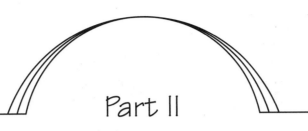

Part II

Lessons and Activities

These seven lessons are designed to deepen children's understanding of the social concepts and skills introduced in *The Rainbow Kids Story.* Each lesson includes objectives, procedures for presenting the lesson, notes to the teacher, and ideas for follow-up activities.

The two activities listed after Lesson 7 are fun extension activities. "Illustrate the Story" can be presented immediately after reading *The Rainbow Kids Story* aloud. In addition to suggestions about how to make a rainbow kids picture book, this activity also presents fun rainbow projects and a list of children's books about rainbows. The last activity, "The Empathy Game" teaches children to tune into the feelings of others and can be played anytime.

Lesson 1
I Feel Sunny; I Feel Cloudy

Purpose
▶ To introduce a simple vocabulary for talking about feelings
▶ To relate the *sunny* and *cloudy* metaphors to students' experiences
▶ To heighten children's awareness of their feelings and the feelings of others

Timing
Day 4

Materials
▶ Sun and cloud (see Appendix A)
▶ Crayons or markers
▶ Drawing paper

Procedure

1. Discuss the *sunny* and *cloudy* terms.
Elicit children's understanding of the metaphors. Say, "The rainbow kids in the story had different feelings. Sometimes they felt *sunny* (hold up sun) and sometimes they felt *cloudy* (hold up cloud). We have feelings like the rainbow kids. Have you ever felt *sunny*? What do you think *sunny* means? Can you think of a time when you felt *cloudy*? What does *cloudy* mean to you?"

Note: When children first learn about feelings, it's helpful to use these simple terms. *Sunny* refers to feelings that are likely to be present when needs are satisfied and includes happiness, excitement, contentment, gratitude, and delight. *Cloudy* describes feelings that arise when needs are not satisfied, such as anger, sadness, frustration, hurt, and fear. Although children may add "bad" to the list of *cloudy* emotions, avoid using this word yourself. Because "bad" has a double meaning, children may incorrectly assume that there is something bad or wrong about upsetting emotions.

Note: Although most children are eager to talk about *cloudy* feelings, a few may insist that they never experience upsetting emotions. Some deny these emotions because they equate feeling bad with being bad or wrong—perhaps that's because they tend to get in trouble when they feel bad (e.g., angry). We want children to learn that there is nothing bad about the uncomfortable range of emotions, though there are unskillful ways of expressing those feelings.

Children often deny upset feelings because adults act that way. Seligman (1995) points out, in his discussion of our "feel-good" culture, that we tend to banish or minimize negative emotion because we equate success with feeling happy and having high self-esteem. When children feel bad, we instinctively rush to make things better. Although it is natural to want to avoid uncomfortable feelings, there are good reasons to feel bad. Negative emotion alerts us of a problem and motivates us to do something to alleviate the discomfort. We can either relieve the discomfort by staying in the situation and acting in a way that changes it, or we can get rid of the unpleasant feeling by giving up and leaving the situation. The first tactic Seligman calls mastery, the second he calls learned help-lessness. Mastery begins by increasing children's awareness of their upsetting emotions (in this lesson and in Lesson 3), and their choices for healthy expression (Lessons 4–7).

2. Introduce the activity.

Distribute paper and art supplies. Tell students, "Let's find out about your feelings. Fold your paper in half. At the top of one side draw a sun. Under the sun draw a picture of a time you felt *sunny*." Give an example and elicit examples from the children.

Continue, "On the other side of the paper, draw a cloud at the top. Under the cloud draw a picture of a time you felt *cloudy*." Again, offer an example of your own and elicit additional examples from the children. Point out that feeling *cloudy* is a normal part of life and that everyone feels *cloudy* at times.

3. Help children write or dictate a sentence about their pictures.

Circulate among the children and talk with them about their pictures. As they write or dictate their stories, ask them to begin with these sentence starters: "I feel sunny when . . ." or "I feel cloudy when . . . ."

4. Set up a time for children to share their *sunny* and *cloudy* pictures with the class.

Point out how we are alike and how we are different. For example, "Everyone has feelings. We all feel *sunny* at times and *cloudy* at times. What makes me feel *sunny* and *cloudy* may be different from what makes you feel *sunny* and *cloudy*. Evan loves playing chase at recess. When someone chases Evan, he feels *sunny*. But Hannah feels *cloudy* whenever people run after her."

You may wish to bind the papers together and make a class book that children can read and enjoy.

Ideas for Living the Lessons

Teacher Ideas

Julie Johnson has a Monday morning sharing ritual called Weekend News. During circle time her Kindergarteners are invited to talk about recent *sunny* and *cloudy* happenings. As the children share, they hold up either a sun or a cloud symbol. Once, Julie followed the discussion with art and language activities. The children drew pictures of their *sunny* and *cloudy* stories with black markers on construction paper—white paper for *sunny* stories and gray paper for *cloudy* ones. The kids then colored the pictures with crayons or oil pastels and painted them with a light watercolor wash of yellow or gray. Finally, the children dictated sentences describing their crayon-resist creations.

Barbara Fong, a Kindergarten teacher in Atherton, California, has her children share their *sunny* and *cloudy* feelings on separate days. The class sits in a circle and either a cloud or a sun is passed around to indicate whose turn it is to speak. The sun symbol is made from two paper plates painted yellow and stapled together, with construction paper rays stapled around the edges. Cut a cloud shape from two gray pieces of construction paper, staple them together around the edges and stuff them with newspaper to make a puffy cloud.

Note: As children share their *sunny* and *cloudy* pictures, they discover that everyone has individual emotional responses. This concept eventually leads to the understanding that, in order to interact with someone in a positive way, it is important to consider that person's feelings. Perspective taking and empathy skills are further developed in Lesson 2 and in the Empathy Game at the end of Part II.

Lesson 1 Reading List

Children's Books About Feelings

Aliki (see Brandenberg)

Berry, J. (2000). *Let's talk about feeling disappointed.* New London, NC: Gold Star Publishing. (disappointment)

Bourgeois, P. (1986). *Franklin in the dark.* New York: Scholastic Inc. (fear)

Brandenberg, A. (1982). *We are best friends.* New York: Greenwillow Books (loneliness)

Brandenberg, A. (1984). *Feelings.* New York: Greenwillow Books. (various feelings)

Carlson, N. (1982). *Harriet's recital.* Minneapolis: Carolrhonda Books. (nervousness)

Carlson, N. (1989). *Arnie and the stolen markers.* New York: Viking Kestrel. (guilt, remorse)

Curtis, J. L. (1998). *Today I feel silly.* New York: HarperCollins Publishers. (various feelings)

Emberley, E. (1992). *Go away, big green monster!* Boston: Little, Brown and Co. (fear)

Fox, M. (1989). *Koala Lou.* San Diego: Harcourt, Brace, Jovanovich. (love)

Freeman, D. (1968). *Corduroy.* New York: Viking Press. (love)

Freymann, S., & Elffers, J. (1999). *How are you peeling; food with moods.* New York: Arthur A Levine Books. (various feelings)

Henkes, K. (1991). *Chrysanthemum.* New York: Greenwillow Books. (embarrassment)

Henkes, K. (1987). *Sheila Rae, the brave.* New York: Greenwillow Books. (bravery)

Henkes, K. (1990). *Julius, the baby of the world.* New York: Greenwillow Books. (anger, jealousy)

Henkes, K. (1993). *Owen.* New York: Greenwillow Books. (insecurity)

Henkes, K. (1996). *Lily's purple plastic purse.* New York: Greenwillow Books. (regret)

Henkes, K. (2000). *Wemberly worried.* New York: Greenwillow Books. (worry)

Hest, A. (1995). *In the rain with baby duck.* Cambridge, MA: Candlewick Press. (grumpiness)

Hoban, R. (1968). *A birthday for Frances.* New York: HarperCollins Publishers. (jealousy)

Lionni, L. (1969). *Alexander and the wind-up mouse.* New York: Pantheon. (jealousy)

Matsuno, M. (1960). *A pair of red clogs.* Cleveland, OH: World Publishing Co. (regret)

Mayer, M. (1974). *You're the scaredy-cat.* New York: Four Winds Press. (fear)

Parr, T. (2000). *The feelings book.* Boston: Little, Brown and Co. (various feelings)

Showers, P. (1977). *A book of scary things.* New York: Doubleday. (fear)

Simon, N. (1974). *I was so mad!* Morton Grove, IL: Albert Whitman. (anger)

Simon, N. (1988). *I am not a crybaby.* Morton Grove, IL: Albert Whitman. (sadness)

Viorst, J. (1972). *Alexander and the terrible, no good very bad day.* New York: Scholastic. (frustration)

Waber, B. (1972). *Ira sleeps over.* Boston: Houghton Mifflin. (fear)

Wells, R. (1988). *Shy Charles.* New York: Dial Books. (bashfulness)

Williams, V. (1982). *A chair for my mother.* New York: Greenwillow Books. (love)

Zolotow, C. (1976). *It's not fair.* New York: HarperCollins Publishers. (jealousy)

Lesson 2
We Spread Sunshine

Purpose
- To relate the *spreading sunshine* metaphor to children's experience
- To heighten children's awareness of the positive effects of caring
- To give children practice *spreading sunshine*, that is, empathizing with others and showing kindness to others

Timing
Day 5

Materials
- Examples of *spreading sunshine* behavior (collected beforehand)
- We Spread Sunshine chart (described in this lesson plan)
- Large sun (see Appendix A)

Procedure

1. Make charts for the next three lessons.
Observe students ahead of time and jot down three or four examples of *spreading sunshine, feeling cloudy,* and *clearing clouds away.* Note who is involved and what happened in each incident. Use this information to prepare the three charts that follow. The chart, We Spread Sunshine, is used in this lesson. The We Feel Cloudy chart will be used in Lesson 3 and the We Clear Clouds Away chart will be used in Lessons 4–7. When recording *cloudy* incidents that involve more than one child, use the indefinite "someone" instead of the name of the person who was hurtful, as shown on the We Feel Cloudy chart.

Note: Here's a chance for children to try out and develop the social skills that offer caring and support to others. As children identify acts of kindness and consider how the gesture will be received, they develop the skill of empathy. *Spreading sunshine* also contributes to the development of a respectful, loving classroom community.

Note: Conventional wisdom would have us praise children whenever they are kind so that they will continue these positive behaviors. Comments like, "That was so nice of you, Rachel," however, can actually detract from the lesson being taught. We want children to associate their caring gestures with the positive feeling they automatically get when they are kind to others, not with winning public recognition or the teacher's approval. This is a subtle but important distinction. The practice of rewarding desirable social behavior is based on the assumption that children are inherently self-centered and will act generously only when reinforced to do so. However, the opposite is actually true. According to Fabes, Fultz, Eisenberg, May-Plumlee, and Christopher (1989), and Grusec (1991), children who are frequently rewarded for helpfulness tend to be somewhat less generous and cooperative than those who aren't rewarded. That's because the primary lesson the rewarded child learns is that if he is caring, he will get something in return. When the goodies are

Sample Charts

We Spread Sunshine

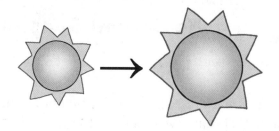

) Rachel shared her snack with Lizzy.
) Jasper gave Erin a tissue.

We Feel Cloudy

) Someone called Raymond a name.
) Silvia's gerbil died.

We Clear Clouds Away

) Theresa picked up Evan's book when she knocked it off the desk.
) Stephan said "sorry" when he spilled Audrey's juice.

2. Introduce and discuss the *spreading sunshine* metaphor.
Tell students, "The rainbow kids were good at *spreading sunshine* at the beginning of the story. What does *spreading sunshine* mean?" Any action, word, or gesture that lets others know you care about them is *spreading sunshine*.

3. Help children identify ways they *spread sunshine* to each other.
Say, "I have noticed we are like the rainbow kids. Sometimes we *spread sunshine* too."

Display the first chart and read the examples listed. After each example, invite the child or children named in the incident to talk about their feelings. For instance, in the lesson-plan example noted on the We Spread Sunshine chart, the teacher would say, "Lizzy, how did you feel when Rachel shared her snack with you? Rachel, how did you feel when you gave some of your snack to Lizzy?" Use children's answers to point out that *spreading sunshine* often leads to more positive feelings for both people. "When you *spread sunshine,* your sun tends to grow bigger and so does the sun of the other person."

After reading the examples written on the chart, elicit other examples of *spreading sunshine.* Ask, "Has anyone else noticed *spreading sunshine* in our class? Are there times when you *spread sunshine* to someone? Has anyone *spread sunshine* to you?" Quickly jot down the children's anecdotes; add their examples to the chart later. Each time a child offers an example, nod and reply matter-of-factly, "Yes, that's *spreading sunshine.*" Avoid complimenting or praising the child who showed the kindness.

The purpose of the lesson is not to reward caring children with public attention, although that will happen inadvertently in this activity, but to acknowledge kind deeds and their effects.

4. Continue exploring the concept of *spreading sunshine.*
Invite children to report *sunny* incidents as they occur.

Keep track and add the new examples to the chart. Read the new entries daily. Continue collecting and recording *spreading sunshine*

gone, so is the inclination to care. Rewards teach children compliance, not altruism.

The *Rainbow Kids Program* is based on the optimistic belief that children are as capable of generosity and empathy as they are of self-centeredness. (Literature supporting this assumption is extensively reviewed in Kohn, 1990.) When teachers treat children as if they are capable of acting virtuously and trust them to do so, students fulfill this positive prophecy. Children who are unkind and fall short of their capacity to care are viewed as students needing guidance, not as inherently selfish children. The teacher's task is to work with the thoughtless child to help him see the effects of his unkind behavior and learn a more positive way of handling the situation next time.

Note: Sue Sartor noticed that occasionally a few of her Kindergarten children would compete to have their names written the most times on the We Spread Sunshine chart. The game was cut short when she asked children to report only what others had done for them, not what they had done for others.

Note: Caring Time is a wonderful activity to close the day. It is simple and quick enough for everyone to take a turn, it creates good feelings in the room, and it ends the day on a high note. It also shows that acknowledging kindness is another way to *spread sunshine* and demonstrates the principle that when you *spread sunshine* to someone, you are likely to receive *sunshine* in return.

Initially children use Caring Time to thank one or more people for "being my friend" or "playing with me at recess." Eventually challenge students to be more specific, "What is it about Audrey that lets you know she is your friend? What does she do or say?" With practice, children become increasingly perceptive, thoughtful, and appreciative of the kindnesses they experience throughout the day.

anecdotes until everyone is listed on the chart at least once. (Don't forget to include yourself.) Every child needs to feel part of the caring classroom community. If you find that a few children have not been named, privately coach them to think of a kind gesture and support them to carry it out.

5. Phase out charting *spreading sunshine* incidents as children internalize the concept.

Say, "As I look at the chart, I see that everyone understands what *spreading sunshine* means. Now that we all know how to *spread sunshine* we won't keep track on the chart anymore."

6. If you wish to continue acknowledging *spreading sunshine*, begin a Caring Time ritual.

Caring Time gives children practice reflecting on their experiences and expressing appreciation to others.

Explain, "We are going to start a new activity to thank others who recently *spread sunshine* to us. It's called Caring Time. We'll sit in a circle and pass around this sun. If you want to care about someone, wait until the sun is passed to you and then say, 'I'd like to thank _____ (name(s)) for _____ (specific behavior).'" Until children learn what to say, write the sentence on a strip of paper. Continue, "For example, my arms were full when I arrived this morning and Theresa opened the door for me. So, I would say, 'I'd like to thank Theresa for holding the door open for me.' Does anyone else want to try?" Pass the sun to those who volunteer to express thanks.

Ideas for Living the Lessons

Spreading sunshine book

Invite children to help write and illustrate a page in a classroom book, *We Spread Sunshine*. Explain, "On each page include an example of a time you *spread sunshine* to someone and a time someone *spread sunshine* to you." Collect the pages, punch holes on one side and bind the pages together.

Sunshine board

Set up a Sunshine Board in your room, a place for reverse graffiti. Post yellow butcher paper and invite children to write *sunny* comments about their classmates. For example, "Marco saved me a seat. — Charles."

Rainbow chain

Each time children in your class *spread sunshine,* invite them to add a rainbow colored link to a paper chain. Drape the chain around the room.

Sunny songs

Singing creates happy feelings and builds a sense of community. Learn songs that emphasize *sunny* themes and relate the lyrics to the principles you are studying. (There are several songs with *sunny* themes in Appendix E.) For example, in "The Magic Penny," discuss how the penny and sunshine are both metaphors for love. If you introduce the songs while you are learning about *spreading sunshine,* children will associate the songs with the warm feelings they experienced when they first learned about expressing kindness.

Incorporate the *sunny* term and concept into daily classroom life.

Look for natural opportunities to notice or elicit *spreading sunshine* behavior. For example, when characters in a story show kindness, pause and say, "That's *spreading sunshine.*" At the end of a game, ask the winning team to think of *sunny* ways to interact with the other team. Before a new student enters the class, invite children to brainstorm ways to *spread sunshine* to her and help her feel welcome. Valentine's Day and Mother's Day can be presented as special days to show kindness and gratitude to those we care about.

Sunny words (good manners)

While passing out papers one day, it wasn't until I was halfway around the room that I heard a child say, "thank you." I automatically paused and said, "That's *spreading sunshine.*" Everybody after that, of course, expressed thanks. (In fact it got so *sunny* in the room I had to put on my sunglasses, a response I reserved for especially bright moments.) This began a discussion about simple words we can use to let others know we care about them. We discovered that the *way* we speak can also express our consideration (or disregard) for the other person and that people are more likely to respond positively when we use *sunny* words and a pleasant tone of voice. I demonstrated with an example. "I'm going to say something two different ways. Tell me which way you like best. Give me that pencil (bossy tone)! Or, may I please have the pencil (pleasant tone)?"

Next, I read children's books about manners that pointed out other examples of polite social behavior. (See the Reading List at the end of this lesson.) The more we focused on courteous behavior, the more polite words were used in the classroom and the more firmly established good manners became as a habit. Our study ended by making a Sunny Words Mobile that included please, thank you, you're welcome, excuse me, I'm sorry, and may I.

Spread sunshine beyond the classroom.

Broaden children's understanding of altruism. Beautify the school, collect and donate used toys to a homeless shelter, sing songs at a nursing home or recycle paper scraps to *spread sunshine* to others and to the environment.

Expand children's emotion-related vocabulary beyond the simple *sunny* term.

Once children have mastered the idea that some feelings are *sunny*, introduce feeling words that describe a full range of positive emotions. Make a Sunny Feelings chart and brainstorm a list of pleasant emotions. Talk about events that might trigger the feeling and describe how the emotion feels. Share stories of your own. For example, "On the night before my birthday I would sometimes feel so excited that I could hardly sleep. When I thought about the fun I was going to have, I felt bouncy and energetic and like I couldn't wait for tomorrow to get here. What are some times you have felt excited?" Keep the Sunny Feelings chart on the wall and continue adding words as new feelings come up—in stories or in real life events. Encourage children to talk about their feelings using the words on the chart.

Make feelings a legitimate topic of conversation by sharing feelings of your own. For example, "I appreciate how quickly you cleaned the room today!"

Teacher Ideas

Sandy Sale, who teaches Kindergarten in Atherton, California, made a giant *spreading sunshine* sun with her class. Every time someone *spread sunshine*, they wrote the kind deed on a ray and added it to the sun.

Amy Jue, a 2nd grade teacher in Foster City, California, created a Rainbow Kids Corner in her room. In the corner were the books they had made from earlier lessons (The Rainbow Kids Book they illustrated and the I Feel Sunny, I Feel Cloudy Book), a poster showing children's faces with different emotions, and a mailbox. When children observed something *sunny*, they filled out and "mailed" a special note recording the date, names of the children involved, and a description of what happened. After lunch, Amy opened the mail and read the entries aloud as she invited the class to clap in appreciation of the *sunny* deeds.

In Roosevelt School in Redwood City, California, where all the primary classrooms were studying *Rainbow Kids* at the same time, the children added a link to a paper rainbow chain whenever *spreading sunshine* occurred. The chain, which was draped around the room, eventually went out the door and linked all the classrooms together.

Gerry Thompson's Kindergarten students and their 3rd grade buddies at Las Lomitas Elementary *spread sunshine* to the school by cleaning the lunch benches. Also, on May Day her children *spread sunshine* throughout the school neighborhood by hanging May baskets filled with handmade flowers on neighbors' doorknobs, ringing the bell, and running away.

Lesson 2 Reading List

Children's Books About Manners

Aliki (see Brandenberg)

Berenstain, S., & Berenstain, J. (1985). *The Berenstain bears forget their manners.* New York: Random House.

Brandenberg, Aliki. (1990). *Manners.* New York: Greenwillow Books.

Bridwell, N. (1986). *Clifford's manners.* New York: Scholastic Inc.

Carlson, N. (1994). *How to lose all your friends.* New York: Viking Press.

Cole, J. (1985). *Monster manners.* New York: Scholastic Inc.

Hoban, R. (1966). *The little brute family.* New York: Macmillan.

Joslin, S. (1958). *What do you say, dear?* New York: Young Scott Books.

Joslin, S. (1961). *What do you do, dear?* New York: Young Scott Books.

Parrish, P. (1978). *Mind your manners.* New York: Greenwillow Books.

Scarry, R. (1973). *Please and thank you book.* New York: Random House.

Zolotow, C. (1963). *The quarreling book.* New York: HarperCollins.

Children's Books About Helpfulness and Care of the Earth

Berenstain, S., & Berenstain, J. (1991). *The Berenstain bears don't pollute anymore.* New York: Random House.

Berenstain, S., & Berenstain, J. (1998). *The Berenstain bears lend a helping hand.* New York: Random House.

Berry, J. (1996). *Let's talk about being helpful.* New York: Scholastic Inc.

Bridwell, N. (1975). *Clifford's good deed.* New York: Four Winds Press.

Burningham, J. (1990). *Hey! Get off our train.* New York: Crown Publishers.

De Paola, T. (1975). *Michael bird-boy.* New York: Prentice-Hall.

DiSalvo-Ryan, D. (1991). *Uncle Willie and the soup kitchen.* New York: Morrow Junior Books.

Franklin, K. (1994). *When the monkeys came back.* New York: Atheneum.

Gibbons, G. (1992). *Recycle! A handbook for kids.* Boston: Little, Brown and Co.

Hallinan, P.K. (1992). *For the love of our earth.* Nashville, TN: Ideals Children's Books.

Hoose, P., & Hoose, H. (1998). *Hey, little ant.* Berkeley, CA: Tricycle Books.

Janovitz, M. (1996). *Can I help?* New York: North-South Books.

Markova, D. (1994). *Kids random acts of kindness.* Berkeley, CA: Conari Press.

Ray, M. L. (1996). *Pumpkins: A story for a field.* Orlando, FL: Harcourt Brace.

Rose, D. (1990). *The people who hugged trees.* Niwot: CO: Roberts Rinehart.

Seuss, Dr. (1971). *The lorax.* New York: Random House.

Steig, W. (1971). *Amos and Boris.* New York: Farrar, Straus, and Giroux.

Woods, A. (2000). *Jubal's wish.* New York: Blue Sky Press.

Yoshi, A. C. (1988). *Big Al.* New York: Scholastic Inc.

Zolotow, C. (1958). *Do you know what I'll do?* New York: HarperCollins
Publishers.

Teacher's Resource

The Random Acts of Kindness Foundation has a free teacher's guide
that gives information about bringing kindness into the curriculum.
Visit their Web site at www.actsofkindness.org.

Lesson 3
We Feel Cloudy

Purpose
▶ To introduce a simple vocabulary for talking about unpleasant emotions
▶ To relate the *cloudy* metaphor to children's experience
▶ To increase children's awareness and acceptance of their own upsetting feelings and those of others

Timing
Day 6

Materials
▶ Examples of *cloudy* incidents collected beforehand and recorded on the We Feel Cloudy chart (described in Lesson 2)
▶ Cloud (see Appendix A)

Procedure

1. Introduce and discuss the *cloudy* metaphor.
Say to students, "Sometimes the rainbow kids felt *cloudy*. (Hold up cloud.) Can you remember what happened in the story that caused the kids to feel *cloudy*? What do you think *cloudy* means?"

Note: The *cloudy* metaphor refers to any unpleasant emotion, including anger, frustration, fear, or sadness. *Cloudy* feelings accompany unmet needs and are sometimes caused by the uncaring or hurtful actions of others.

2. Help children identify and explore their *cloudy* feelings.

Say to students, "I have noticed that sometimes we feel *cloudy*, too, just like the rainbow kids." Give an example of a time you felt *cloudy* recently. This lets children know that everyone experiences upsetting emotions at times, even grown-ups. For instance, "I was waiting for a parking place and a car pulled in front of me and took the space I wanted. I felt *cloudy* when that person cut ahead of me and took my place."

Next, read the examples you recorded earlier on the We Feel Cloudy chart. Invite the child named to talk about the experience. For instance, "Yesterday someone called Raymond a name. Raymond, how did you feel when that happened?" Use the student's answer to explore the hurt feelings and investigate the causes. If the *cloudy* incident involves another child, ask the student to use the word "someone" rather than the name of the child who *threw the cloud*.

The purpose of the activity is to identify and explore *cloudy* feelings, not to identify children who were hurtful in the past. If there were retaliatory actions, discuss the outcome. Ask, "What happened next? When *clouds* are *thrown* back, does that make the problem bigger or smaller?" Point out to children that, although retaliatory actions feel right in the moment, they usually lead to negative consequences. As demonstrated in the story, the problem (and the *cloud* cover) grows bigger for everyone and becomes more difficult to resolve.

3. Elicit other examples of *cloudy* feelings.

Ask, "Has anyone else felt *cloudy*? What happened? If someone else is involved, start your story with 'someone' instead of the person's name."

As children report, paraphrase what they say and jot down the anecdotes. Add the examples to the chart later. Read the new entries daily.

4. Continue collecting examples of *cloudy* feelings and adding them to the chart.

Keep your clipboard handy and record children's reports about their *cloudy* feelings. Listen to the upset child and restate what you heard,

Note: When other children are involved in precipitating *cloudy* feelings, it is important not to publicly name the child who was hurtful. Though most children probably know or could easily guess the person who *threw the cloud*, pointing a finger at that child could seriously backfire. The accused child is likely to feel *cloudier* and become either defensive and aggressive, or withdrawn and embarrassed. Keeping track of the children who *throw clouds* also implies that these children are bad, a prophecy that discouraged children are very capable of fulfilling. The idea we want to communicate is that there are unskillful ways of expressing feelings that anyone is capable of.

There may be a child in the class who identifies with the Zeke character or is identified by others as being "just like Zeke." If that happens, point out that Zeke was not different from the rainbow kids. Zeke had a sun, just like the rainbow kids. The rainbow kids *threw clouds*, just like Zeke. No one is bad, though there are unskillful ways of expressing upset (*cloudy*) feelings.

Incidentally, the information on the We Feel Cloudy chart is not lost on the anonymous children who *threw* the *clouds*. By the end of this lesson everyone is clear about the behaviors others find hurtful. In the next three lessons children also learn that when they feel *cloudy*, and that is likely to happen, they can *clear the clouds away* rather than *throw them back*.

Note: Now that it is safe for children to talk about their upset feelings, they will have no trouble keeping you informed about all the bad things that happen. You may be overwhelmed by the quantity of *cloudy* feelings reported. Although this might feel like you have just opened Pandora's Box of Tattled Tales, remember this is only the first step in helping children become independent problem solvers. Think of the children's reports not as "tattled tales" in which you are obliged to right the wrong, but as requests for you to coach and support them to *clear clouds away*.

Realize that children who report their *cloudy* feelings are already a couple steps into the problem-solving process. They are demonstrating their awareness of unhappy feelings, and they are choosing to communicate to you *rather* than engaging in battle. (No doubt a few will fight, then tell, but if they are interrupting their usual round of *cloud throwing*, this still represents some progress.) Telling the teacher succeeds in slowing the process down, putting some air time between a hurtful action and the usual *cloudy* reaction. It is in this space that children will eventually stop and remember to *clear clouds away*.

both the child's feelings and the precipitating event. When the incident is reported privately, it is not necessary to protect the identity of the child who *threw the cloud*, though continue using the generic "someone" on the chart. (In the case of a serious offense, you need to know who was hurtful so you can quickly intervene.) Add the examples to the chart later.

5. Discontinue charting *cloudy* feelings.

When you have gathered a representative sample of *cloudy* feelings and the hurtful behaviors that are occurring in your classroom, phase out recording the incidents on the We Feel Cloudy chart.

NIX THE "NO TATTLING" RULE

Young children are notorious for running to the teacher to report every little thing that goes wrong in the room. Understandably, teachers grow weary of these interruptions, most of which are about trivial matters. In an effort to cut down on tattled tales, many teachers establish a "No Tattling" policy. Tattling, it is often explained, is when a child reports something to the teacher that does not directly involve him. (Asking a teacher for help about a problem the child is having, on the other hand, is usually considered acceptable, though some teachers insist that children not tattle about their own problems. These teachers want children to handle their problems by themselves, but most children can't do that until we teach them how.)

The problem with the "No Tattling" rule is that it isn't always appropriate. Teachers need to hear about the student who scribbled on the bathroom wall or the student who is being cruel on the playground, or the student who brought a weapon to school. In a "No Tattling" classroom, law-abiding youngsters may hesitate to tell about these disturbing events because they aren't "directly involved." This cuts teachers off from their quickest and most reliable source of information about what's going on at school—other students. In these uncertain and dangerous times, we cannot afford to do that.

The "No Tattling" rule also puts children in a precarious position. If a student hears about a potentially dangerous situation and fails to report it, that student is in big trouble if something does happen and people get hurt. Teachers try to correct for this by insisting students report any "serious" problem. But what's serious to a grown-up may not seem serious to a child. Even some adults have been tricked into thinking that threatening talk was "just kidding around."

Another popular way of stating the "deciding when to tell" clause is equally problematic. Before coming to the teacher the child is asked to consider this: "Does the situation really concern you or are you just trying to get someone into trouble?" Or, "Are you trying to hurt someone or help someone?" This is a hard question for the child because it is not up to him what happens next. The most honest answer is, "Well, teacher, that depends on whether you're going to

(continued on page 104)

Note: Even after you stop recording *cloudy* incidents on the chart, children will, of course, continue to report upsetting events. How should you respond? Eventually you will guide children to take steps to solve the problem. Meanwhile, most children do not yet have the skills to *clear clouds away* (the subject of Lessons 4–7) and it can be awkward to proceed. One effective response is to let the child know you are listening and that you care. It's best to nod and paraphrase what the child said, both the feelings and what happened. For example, when Sammy reports a pencil problem, say, "So, you're feeling upset because Cherie took your pencil. Yes, that's a *cloud.*" You might also go a step further and suggest to Sammy, "Tell Cherie how you feel and what you want." Sammy could be encouraged to tell Cherie, "I felt *cloudy* when you took my pencil. Please give it back." Although this is the assertive speaking skill that will be introduced in Lesson 6, there's no reason to wait if you can easily coach the child to take the next step.

The two things you want to avoid, although these may be your most automatic responses, are telling children not to tattle and quickly stepping in and handling the situation yourself. The "No Tattling Rule" is downright dangerous because it prevents us from finding out about potentially hurtful or unsafe situations. For more information, see Nix the 'No Tattling' Rule, pp. 102—104.

Settling the matter yourself, "Cherie, give Sammy back his pencil!" quickly fixes the situation but perpetuates a cycle in which children do not take responsibility for handling their problems and teachers get worn out listening to tattled tales and coming up with solutions.

This is not to say we should never intervene when children present us with problems. There are many situations that warrant our immediate involvement. When Kristin reports that Andre is chasing Mary with a stick, give a loud command, "Andre, put the stick down!" I am simply suggesting that we use less serious problems, those that children are capable of handling, to teach problem-solving skills.

It is difficult to invite children to "tell" at a time when they have not yet developed the skills to resolve problems on their own. But keep your eye on the horizon. Having elicited a long list of *cloudy* feelings, everyone, including you, will feel a real need to learn the next lessons well.

punish the kid or use this as an opportunity to help him change." But most children just shrug their shoulders and walk away.

Children get into another kind of trouble when they follow the rule and only report matters that concern them. While many teachers say it is okay to tell about problems that happen to them, children don't see it that way. If Theresa tells the teacher, "Luis called me a bad name" and Luis gets a scolding, Luis may still call her a tattletale, which is the worse name of all. Theresa eventually figures out that, regardless of the teacher's definition, "tattling" is synonymous with telling the teacher anything that might get someone into trouble. When a classmate is mean to Theresa after that, she must choose between getting the teacher involved and facing backlash from tattling, or keeping the matter to herself.

I say forget the "No Tattling" rule and the word "tattletale" altogether. Listen to what children have to say, consider the information and the source and decide how best to proceed. The child who is in your face 10 times a day reporting every tiny transgression may need to be taught to ask for attention in more acceptable ways. The overly sensitive child who takes offense at the slightest provocation needs to learn not to sweat the small stuff. The child who tries to coerce others with the threat, "I'm telling," needs to realize that the teacher is not a punishing agent, but rather a coach that will support him to solve his own problems. The "teller" who is a responsible citizen reporting the violation of an important rule needs to know the teacher can be trusted to take immediate action and right the wrong. In each case the teacher makes the call and chooses a response that is appropriate to the student and the situation.

Every time children come to us, they are asking us to listen. When we cut them short with "don't tattle," we not only miss important information and the chance to teach new skills, but we give children the message that we don't care about some of their concerns (though it is fuzzy which ones). This message is antithetical to the goals of a social skills program. Children won't learn to care about others if we treat them as if we don't care about them.

Ideas For Living the Lessons

Notice and discuss *cloudy* feelings as they arise in daily classroom life.

Make it emotionally safe to talk about *cloudy* feelings. Take time to discuss the situations your students disclose. For example, when a child reports that his pet died, listen with your full attention and let him know you understand and care. Talk about the sadness and sense of loss he may be feeling. Offer extra hugs and comfort that day (at the child's request). Be aware that there is nothing to *do* about feelings related to grief or loss. Although it is natural to want to cheer the child up with a comment like, "Now you can get a new kitten," it is better to simply let the child experience the feelings and process them in his own way. You may even want to remind the child that it's okay to feel *cloudy*.

Read stories that explore *cloudy* feelings.

There are many children's books that deal with emotional issues and offer an excellent springboard for discussing a wide range of emotions (see Children's Books About Feelings, pp. 89–90). For example, when a character in a story is sad, ask, "How do you think Corduroy felt when he lost his button?" When characters are hurtful, pause and say, "That's *throwing a cloud*. Did that make the problem bigger or smaller? What do you think will happen next?"

Narrate a *storm* as it occurs.

When *cloudy* incidents occur in the room, talk about what is happening and reinforce the idea that *throwing clouds* often makes the problem bigger for everyone. Here is an example of how I used a real-life problem to point out the negative effects of *cloud throwing* behavior and to find a better way to solve the problem.

Finding a seat at circle time often causes problems as everyone scrambles to sit by a favorite person. Once, while watching two boys struggle to sit on the same chair, I offered a blow-by-blow description of the *storm* as it unfolded. Using a sportscaster voice I quietly reported, "And, it looks like Sammy and Jameil are both trying to sit in the same chair . . . now Sammy is pushing Jameil off the chair . . .

Note: As you continue to explore and chart the emotions that arise in daily classroom life, you may discover that some feelings don't seem to fit on the Sunny or Cloudy Word charts. Create a new chart called Other Feelings and list those feelings that are neither pleasant nor unpleasant, such as sorry, confused, or shy.

now Jameil is yelling at Sammy that he got there first . . . but Sammy is shouting right back that it is HIS chair."

The boys stopped in their tracks when they noticed everyone's rapt attention. "Thanks for stopping the *storm,* Sammy and Jameil," I said. "Let's talk about what just happened." In the discussion that followed, the children reviewed all we had learned about *cloud throwing* and came up with a list of better ways to solve the problem. In the end Sammy and Jameil decided to take turns sitting by their friend, Luis.

Expand children's emotion-related vocabulary beyond the simple *cloudy* term.

Once children have internalized the idea that some feelings are *cloudy,* introduce feeling words that describe a full range of unpleasant emotions. Make a Cloudy Feelings chart and brainstorm a list of feelings that fit in the *cloudy* category. Talk about what triggers each emotion and describe the sensations that accompany the feeling. Share stories of your own. For example, "Once when I was in 3rd grade I had to sing by myself in a school play. During the performance I forgot the words to the song. My face turned red and my ears burned. I wanted to disappear. I felt embarrassed."

Post the Cloudy Feelings chart on the wall and continue adding words as new feelings come up—in stories or in real-life events. Encourage children to use these words when they talk about their experiences and share your own feeling when appropriate. For example, "I'm disappointed that it's raining and we can't go outside." When children report their upsets, paraphrase what they say and guess their feelings. For example, when Audrey reports that her Mom is out of town, respond by saying, "So, you are feeling sad that your Mom is away and you miss not having her at home?"

Teacher Idea

Barbara Fong, a 1st grade teacher in Atherton, California, purchased a commercial poster of feeling words with pictures of children's faces, cut the pictures apart, and invited the children to sort them into *sunny, cloudy* and "other" feeling categories.

Lesson 3 Reading List

Children's Books About Loss and Grieving

Brown, M. W. (1958). *The dead bird.* Reading, MA: Addison-Wesley.

Carrick, C. (1976). *The accident.* New York: Houghton Mifflin.

Clifton, L. (1983). *Everett Anderson's goodbye.* New York: Holt, Rinehart and Winston.

De Paola, T. (1973). *Nana upstairs, Nana downstairs.* New York: Putnam.

Mellonie, B., & Ingpen, R. (1983). *Lifetimes: The beautiful way to explain death to children.* New York: Bantam Books.

Misaka, M. (1971). *Annie and the old one.* Boston: Little, Brown and Co.

Varley, S. (1984). *Badger's parting gifts.* New York: Lothrup, Lee and Shepard Books.

Viorst, J. (1971). *The tenth good thing about Barney.* New York: Atheneum.

Wilhelm, H. (1985). *I'll always love you.* New York: Crown Publishers.

Zolotow, C. (1995). *When the wind stops.* New York: HarperCollins Publishers.

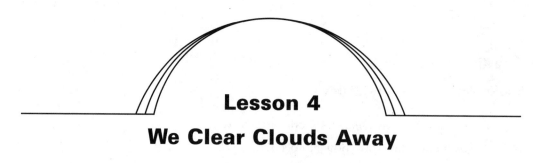

Lesson 4
We Clear Clouds Away

Introducing the Problem-Solving Process

Purpose

▶ To introduce the possibility of expressing *cloudy* or upsetting feelings in ways that lead to positive outcomes

▶ To relate the *clearing clouds away* metaphor to children's experience

▶ To increase children's skill in resolving their interpersonal conflicts, beginning with minor irritations

▶ To introduce "Brainstorm" and "Choose" steps in the problem-solving process

Timing

Day 7

Materials

▶ Examples of *clearing clouds away* incidents collected beforehand and recorded on the We Clear Clouds Away chart (described in Lesson 2)

▶ Sun and cloud with an arrow, the *clearing clouds away* symbol (see Appendix A)

▶ Small cloud and a large sun (see Appendix A)

▶ Light bulb, the symbol for brainstorming (see Appendix A)

▶ Two smiling suns, the symbol for choosing (see Appendix A)

Procedure

1. Introduce and discuss the *clearing clouds away* metaphor.
Say to students, "Remember in *The Rainbow Kids Story* when Julie and Dennis got into a fight during the hide-and-seek game? What did they do that helped *clear the clouds away*? (Hold up the *clearing clouds away* symbol, a sun and cloud with arrow.) What does *clearing clouds away* mean?"

Note: Any word or action that soothes hurt feelings and works to solve the problem is included in the *clearing clouds away* metaphor. Children's answers may include "make up," "say sorry," "be friends," "help each other feel better," "talk about feelings," "talk

108

2. Help children identify ways they *clear clouds away* (solve problems).

Say, "I have noticed that we *clear clouds away* like Julie and Dennis in the story. Sometimes when we get angry or upset, instead of *throwing clouds*, we say or do something that solves the problem and *clears the clouds away*."

Display the We Clear Clouds Away chart and read the examples listed. After each example, invite the two children named in the incident to talk about what happened and how they were feeling. In the example, "Theresa picked up Evan's book when she knocked it off the desk," ask, "Evan, how did you feel when Theresa picked up your book? Theresa, what were you thinking when you picked up Evan's book?" Use children's answers to point out that when *clouds are thrown* (accidental or not) we can *clear them away* by doing something that helps the person feel better and works to solve the problem.

After reading and discussing the examples written on the chart, elicit other examples of problem-solving behavior. Ask, "Has anyone else *cleared clouds away*? What happened? What did you do that helped solve the problem?" If examples are offered, jot them down and add them to the chart. Each time a child gives an example, nod and reply, "Yes, that's *clearing clouds away*." As in the *spreading sunshine* lesson, avoid praising the child who solved the problem. The purpose of the lesson is to explore problem-solving behaviors and their effects, not to single out and compliment individuals who *cleared clouds away*.

3. Continue to elicit examples of *clearing clouds away*.

As in the previous two lessons, invite children to report problem-solving incidents as they occur. Keep track and add the new examples to the chart. Read the new entries daily.

4. Point out the need to learn more about how to *clear clouds away*.

Say, "As I look at our charts, I notice that, even though there are lots of *clouds* in our room (point to the We Feel Cloudy chart), we do not have as many examples of *clearing clouds away*. That may be because it can be difficult to solve problems when we become angry

about the problem," or "find a good solution." In the story, Julie and Dennis solved their problem by talking about what happened and how they were feeling. The *clouds cleared away* when they began expressing concern for one another and when they came up with a solution to Dennis's problem about how he could hide better.

Note: Unlike the We Spread Sunshine and We Feel Cloudy charts, you may have difficulty finding examples of children's problem-solving behavior to write on the chart. This is precisely why you are presenting the *Rainbow Kids Program!* If you come up short, use an adult example from your personal experience or examples of problem-solving behavior you have observed in other children.

and upset. For the next few days, we're going to learn how to *clear clouds away* so that when problems happen in our room (point to the *cloudy* chart), we'll know how to solve them in ways that help everyone feel *sunny* again."

5. Investigate ways to *clear clouds away,* beginning with little clouds (minor irritations).

Say, "Let's start by talking about how to *clear* little *clouds away.* (Hold up a little cloud.) Later we'll learn how to handle bigger problems."

"Little *clouds* happen when we have little problems and when we get a little upset. Often it's easy to think of a way to *clear* a little *cloud away.*" Give an example of a minor problem that occurs in your room and invite children to brainstorm ways to solve it. Have a couple of children act out the scenario as you describe it. Use the symbols when appropriate. Hold up the cloud and sun to show children's feelings. Display the light bulb when children brainstorm, use the smiling suns to indicate when children choose the idea they like best to solve a problem. Here is an example of how I worked with the problem of Raymond taking Chantae's crayon.

I said to the class: "Let's pretend that Chantae is coloring a picture and she leaves her seat to get a drink. While she is gone, her crayon rolls off her desk and Raymond picks it up. When Chantae returns, she notices the crayon in Raymond's hand. How are you feeling, Chantae?"

No doubt Chantae will report that she feels *cloudy,* we hope only a *little cloudy.* Give her a little cloud and discuss the idea that, although Chantae is irritated when she sees that Raymond has her crayon, it is only a little cloud because Chantae can probably think of an easy way to solve the problem.

6. Invite children to brainstorm solutions.

Ask, "What can Chantae do to *clear the cloud away*? (Display the light bulb symbol.) This light bulb means to brainstorm—come up with many ideas, as quickly as possible with no comments." As children offer suggestions, keep track by holding up a finger, one for each idea, or by writing the ideas down. Challenge children to come up with at least a handful of ideas. (That's five.)

For example, "Yes, Chantae could use another crayon. What else could she do? (pause) "Yes, Chantae could ask Raymond to give it back. What else could she do?"

7. Choose an idea that solves the problem and act out the solution.

When children finish naming as many ideas as they can, hold up the symbol for Choose (two smiling suns) and ask Chantae to pick an idea that works to *clear the cloud away*. Chantae, for example, might decide to say to Raymond, "That's my crayon. May I have it back please?" The demonstration ends with Chantae acting out her solution, getting back her crayon, and exchanging her cloud for a sun. Everyone claps to thank the two for demonstrating how to *clear clouds away*.

8. Record the problem-solving example on the We Clear Clouds Away chart.

Although the scenario was contrived by the teacher and resolved in a role-playing exercise, write the children's names and the solution on the chart. In the example above, the teacher would record, "Chantae asked Raymond nicely to return her crayon and Raymond gave it back to her."

9. Present additional demonstrations showing how to *clear clouds away* using situations that commonly occur in your classroom.

Make a list of the little things that go wrong in the room and develop a role-play scenario for each. Select different children to act out the scenarios. Display the weather symbols to show feelings and the Brainstorm and Choose symbols for the appropriate steps. Invite the class to brainstorm many solutions to the problems as described above. Ask the children involved in the demonstration to choose a favorite idea and act it out. Record the winning solutions and the role players on the We Clear Clouds Away chart.

Note: Children get stuck socially because they can think of only one way to solve a problem—MY way! This obvious solution often demands that the other person do all the changing, an idea that is not always acceptable to the other person. When we invite children to brainstorm solutions they discover that there are many ways to solve a problem, some of which work well for both people involved.

Research also underscores the importance of developing children's skill at brainstorming. A study by Shure and Spivack (1982) found that a child's ability to get what he wants in an acceptable way is directly related to the number of different ideas the child can think of in a given situation, and the ability to predict the consequences of those alternatives. The Brainstorm and Choose steps introduced in this role-play activity give children practice in both these skills. These skills are further explored in Lesson 7.

Whenever you invite students to use this divergent thinking tool, hold up the light bulb icon and remind them about the rules for brainstorming—that you are looking for as many different ideas as possible and that all ideas are acceptable. This assures students that it is safe to be creative and that their contributions will not be criticized or judged. (Evaluation of the ideas comes in the next step.) Even silly ideas can lead to creative and workable solutions.

Be careful not to slip and break the no comments rule yourself. When children offer ideas you find unacceptable, resist your temptation to say they are inappropriate. For example, if a child had suggested that Chantae grab the crayon from Raymond, count the idea along with the others, understanding that acknowledging the idea does not necessarily mean you approve of it. Grabbing the crayon *is*, after all, one possibility. It does not work to *clear the cloud away*, however, and will therefore be tossed out in the next step of the process without a word from you.

Note: Here's where children's critical thinking ability comes into play. Choosing a good solution requires children to predict the outcome of each idea and select the idea or ideas that solve the problem in a way that works for everyone.

10. Coach and support children to solve their real-life problems using the script in Appendix D.

Record examples of *clearing clouds away* on the chart whenever children resolve their problems. Ideally everyone's name will eventually appear on the chart at least once.

Ideas for Living the Lesson

Brainstorm solutions to real problems.

The Shure and Spivack study (1982) states that the number of different ideas she has, not the number of good ideas, defines a child's problem-solving ability. It is therefore important to give children lots of practice brainstorming. Real problems are perfect occasions. For example, when a popular book enters the room, say, "Everyone is excited about our new pop-up insect book. Let's brainstorm ways to share the book that are fair to everyone." Sharpen children's brainstorming ability in the regular curriculum as well. For example, in February, children could brainstorm words for a story about Lincoln, or food for a Valentine party. After a big rain, children could hypothesize many possible explanations about why the sidewalk is littered with worms. During math, ask students to brainstorm different combinations to reach the number 10.

Each time you invite children to brainstorm, hold up the light bulb icon and cue them with, "Put on your thinking cap, and let's see how many different ideas we can come up with." Or, "Let's brainstorm. That means to come up with as many different ideas as we can." As children offer ideas, validate their creativity by keeping track of them, either on your fingers or by writing the ideas down.

Clear away accidental clouds.

There are often a few children in the class who automatically take offense when things go wrong or who seem unfamiliar with the idea that accidents happen. Someone gets bumped and we hear, "Stop pushing!" A neighbor uses a stray pencil and is accused of stealing. To make matters worse, the child who caused the accident sometimes reacts to the negative accusation defensively. "You were in my way!" or "I got it first!" and so the *storm* escalates predictably.

After presenting the We Clear Clouds Away lesson, talk about the fact that accidents, unintentional *clouds*, can easily occur and that they often are a source of misunderstanding. Discuss the possibility of quickly *clearing away* an accidental *cloud* by letting the person know it was not done "on purpose." Explain, "You can say something like, 'It was an accident,' or 'Excuse me,' or 'Sorry. I didn't mean to do (specify the action or inaction).' Then, look for ways to *spread sunshine* to that person. Help the person up if you knocked him over. Return the pencil if it belongs to someone else. Ask if he is okay or offer help until you are sure the person has recovered from the mishap, whether physical or emotional."

To bring the lesson home, present a role-play demonstration of an accident and ways to quickly *clear away the* unintended *cloud*. Use the weather symbols to show feelings. Here is an example showing how I helped Silvia and James explore an accidental spill.

I seated Silvia and James across from each other and placed several sizes of suns and clouds on the table between them. Then I told Silvia to accidentally spill some (imaginary) milk on James's side of the table. I said to James, "Let's pretend that you don't know the spill was an accident. How would you probably feel?" James held up a little cloud.

Next, I addressed the class, "Silvia accidentally spilled milk on James's side of the table. Can James tell it was an accident?" In the discussion the children discovered why it might be hard for James to figure out that the spill was accidental just by looking at Silvia. If, for example, Silvia ignored what had just happened, James might think Silvia spilled the milk on purpose. This helped children understand the importance of Silvia taking responsibility for informing James that it was accidental and for helping solve the problem she had unintentionally caused.

"What can you do to *clear the cloud away*?" I asked Silvia. She responded by saying, "Sorry, James, it was an accident." James exchanged his cloud for a sun.

Holding up the light bulb symbol, I invited the class to brainstorm other possibilities. "Are there other things to say or do that might help James feel better about the spilled milk?"

Several children volunteered to demonstrate other *cloud clearing* responses that kept James's sun shining brightly. It was Mandy's response, however, that drew the biggest sun. She ran to the sink, got a paper towel, and cleaned up the spill.

I challenged the children to think a step further. "Even if you weren't the one who caused the accident, can you still help James feel better? How do you think James would feel if two or three children *spread sunshine* to him?"

The children enjoyed the "accident" role-play so much we repeated it with different scenarios a few more times that week. Our practice immediately paid off. When a real accident happened after that, whoever was in the vicinity either coached the child who caused it ("Explain that it was an accident") or expressed concern to the one who was affected by the accident ("Are you all right?"). Once everyone understood how easily accidents happen, they were more willing to assume that mishaps were unintentional and quicker to offer support to *clear the cloud away*. As with other behaviors we were working to establish, the more we practiced handling accidents, the more automatic caring responses became.

Teacher Ideas

In Amy Jue's Rainbow Kids Corner (see the Teacher Ideas section at the end of Lesson 2), children are invited to record *sunny* and *cloudy* incidents on special notes and mail them in a mailbox. The "We Feel Cloudy" notes ask children to record the date, names of the children involved in the *cloudy* incident, a description of the problem, and three ways the *clouds* could have been *cleared away*. After lunch, Amy opens the mail, reads and discusses the *cloudy* entries (without mentioning names) and asks children to think of ways to prevent the problem from happening again. If a serious problem is reported, she talks with those students, privately, at another time. Finally, the *sunny* entries are read aloud to help everyone feel better after all those "*cloudies*."

Julie Johnson's Kindergarteners created their own personal *spreading sunshine, throwing clouds*, and *clearing clouds away* stories using magnetized photos of classmates, magnetized weather symbols, and a magnetic board. (The photos, which were taken with a digital camera, were mounted on stiff paper, cut out and laminated. A piece of magnet tape was then applied to the back of each photo so it would "stick" to the magnet board. The weather symbols were magnetized in the same way.) After a child tells a story to the class, Julie invites a second child to retell the story with a different ending. So, for example, if the first story included a helpful gesture that ended with suns getting bigger, the second version showed a hurtful action that ended with clouds. Julie reported that this storytelling activity heightened children's awareness of the "choice point"—the moment when children decide what action they will take—and the dramatic consequences that follow.

Lesson 5

How to Cool Off

Step 1 of the Problem-Solving Process

Purpose

▶ To help children recognize anger and frustration as feelings that often accompany interpersonal problems

▶ To define cooling off—a way to release upsetting feelings so no one gets hurt—and its importance in solving problems

▶ To help children identify strategies for cooling off

Timing

Day 8

Materials

▶ How to Clear Clouds Away poster (see Appendix D)

▶ Clouds, various sizes (see Appendix A)

▶ Fan, the symbol for Cool Off (see Appendix A)

Procedure

1. Prepare and post the 4-step poster, How to Clear Clouds Away. (Appendix D)

This poster will be used in the next three lessons to introduce the steps in the problem-solving process. Cover the steps with blank paper. As you introduce each step, uncover it on the poster.

2. Explore what happens when intense emotions occur. Investigate the importance of cooling off before attempting to *clear clouds away*.

Say to students, "Yesterday we learned how to *clear* small *clouds away*. Today we're going to talk about how to handle bigger problems." (Hold up a big cloud.)

Continue, "Sometimes problems occur that make us feel so *cloudy*, we have to cool off before we can *clear the clouds away*."

Give an example of a problem that provokes anger or frustration. Ask two children to act out a scenario as you describe it. Here is an example of a conflict that might be used in the demonstration.

Say to students, "Let's pretend that Stephen is working on a puzzle at choice time. Katrina walks over, notices he's doing her favorite puzzle, and stops to watch. Next Katrina picks up a piece and tries to fit it in the puzzle. "Hey!" Stephen shouts, "I'm doing this puzzle!" Katrina shouts back, "Yeah, but I know where this piece goes!" and she moves to put it in. "Stop it!" shouts Stephen and he pushes Katrina aside. In the struggle, they lose their balance, fall on the puzzle and the pieces scatter. How do you think Stephen and Katrina are feeling?" (Give each a big cloud.) "Are Stephen and Katrina ready to *clear the cloud away*? What do you think would happen if they tried to solve the problem right away?"

Point out in the discussion that because they are still so angry, they would probably *throw clouds* and that will only make the problem bigger. Explain, "When we feel very *cloudy* it's important to cool off (hold up fan) before working to solve the problem. After we've had a chance to cool off, we are able to talk more calmly and think more clearly."

3. Explore ways to cool off.

Discuss, "What can Stephen and Katrina do to help themselves feel better? Let's brainstorm ways Stephen and Katrina can cool off (hold up fan) so they will feel calm enough to *clear the cloud away*." Record children's responses on the board.

If unacceptable ideas are named, evaluate the ideas at the end and cross out any harmful ones. Point out, for example, that throwing

Note: Goleman (1995) indicates that when we (children and adults) become very angry or frustrated, we are "emotionally hijacked" by the feeling part of our brain and have no access to our thinking ability. In this highly emotive state we often feel compelled to defend ourselves or impulsively strike back. As *The Rainbow Kids Story* illustrates, saying or doing something hurtful often escalates hostility and makes things worse for everyone. Taking time to cool off helps us refrain from acting impulsively, dissipates our intense emotions and prepares us to think more creatively about solutions.

Note: Any activity that removes or distracts children from the upsetting person or situation can be effective in calming them down. Counting to 10, taking a few deep breaths, getting a drink, doing something physical, drawing a picture, playing with clay, and talking to an understanding person can help dissipate intense emotion. These strategies, however, are less effective when they become habitual (Jensen, 1998). For example, it is quite possible for an adult to count to 10 and continue thinking about an upsetting event. Counting backwards from 100 in Spanish or playing a round of tennis, however, would be more effective and stimulate thinking ability.

In addition to these cooling off strategies, some children benefit from changing the way they think about a situation. According to Seligman (1995), children at risk for depression tend to misinterpret other's intentions and react in harmful, impulsive ways. Girls who tend to be depressed often blame themselves and withdraw when things go wrong ("No one likes me"), while boys are more likely to blame others and become aggressive ("People are out to get me"). Both ways of viewing the world can lead to harmful behavior. Seligman suggests that we teach these children to replace their "hot thoughts" ("people are out to get me") with "cool thoughts" that help them discover more about what happened and consider all the available information before deciding how to respond.

things or yelling loudly are not safe ways to cool off because someone might get hurt, including them. (Excessive yelling damages the vocal chords.)

Add your own cooling off strategies to the list of ideas the children generate.

4. Return to the role-play and invite the two children in the demonstration to choose a cooling off strategy and act it out.

Using the previous example, ask Stephen and Katrina, "What would help you feel better? Which cooling off idea would you like to try?" Katrina might decide to get a drink of water and Stephen might choose to take some deep breaths. After they have each demonstrated a cooling off strategy, ask, "Are you feeling a bit better?" Exchange their big clouds for smaller ones.

Display the How To Clear Clouds Away poster and uncover the first step. Say, "So, we just discovered that when we are very upset and we want to *clear clouds away*, the first step is to stop and cool off."

5. Preview the next lesson.

Tell children, "Now that Stephen and Katrina have cooled off, they are ready to calmly talk about their feelings and about what happened. Tomorrow we will learn how to talk about angry feelings in ways that help *clear the cloud away*."

Ideas for Living the Lessons

I Can Help Myself Feel Better

Using the list of cooling off strategies that you brainstormed with your class (refer to Step 3 of the previous procedures), invite children to draw pictures of their three favorite ways to help themselves feel better. Ask children to dictate or write a story about their pictures. The story can begin, "When I feel cloudy I can make myself feel better. I can ____, ____, or ____." Share the stories with the class. Point out that different people have different ways of managing their upsetting feelings. Let children know that you expect them to use cooling off strategies at school when they become *cloudy* so that they will be better prepared to *clear clouds away.*

Feelings Place

Establish a private place in your room where children can release their emotions in ways that don't hurt or disturb others. Ask children for suggestions about what to put in the Feelings Place that would help them feel better (e.g., a throw rug to define the area, beanbag chair or rocker, tissues for crying, clay, a pad of paper and crayons, blanket, stuffed animal, book). Invite students to use the special place whenever they need to release *cloudy* emotions.

Model Cooling Off

The next time you become angry or frustrated, say that you need to cool off before you proceed. You can combine this information with an I-message, the assertive-speaking skill introduced in the next lesson. For example, "I feel angry when you run back to the classroom from P.E. I'm going to take three deep breaths to cool off and then we'll talk about what happened." This demonstrates that everyone becomes upset at times and shows children how to effectively handle these emotions. Letting students know you are upset and inviting them to cool off with you also gives them a chance to settle down as well.

Lesson 5 Reading List

Children's Books About Cooling Off

Berry, J. (1996). *Let's talk about feeling angry.* New York: Scholastic Inc.

Berry, J. (2000). *Let's talk about feeling frustrated.* New London, NC: Gold Star Publishing.

Crary, E. (1992). *I'm frustrated.* Seattle, WA: Parenting Press, Inc.

Crary, E. (1992). *I'm mad.* Seattle, WA: Parenting Press, Inc.

Everitt, B. (1992). *Mean soup.* New York: Harcourt Brace and Company.

Note: Although many young children quickly process emotions and do not need an elaborate cooling off procedure, a few may benefit from having a private place to release upsetting emotion. Establishing a safe space for intense emotions also reinforces the idea that, while it is okay to be angry and frustrated (*cloudy*), it is not okay to hurt others.

The Feelings Place is not the same as a time out chair or other space for disciplinary action. Children choose to use the Feelings Place. If children are sent to the Feelings Place when angry, they may perceive it as punishment, making it more difficult to cool off.

When a Feelings Place is introduced, many children suddenly display intense feelings. As with any new toy in the room, everyone wants a chance to try it out. My remedy is to invite the class, one at a time, to take a turn in the Feelings Place (set an egg timer to be fair). Once the newness wears off, the space is available for processing real emotions.

The chemistry of your class determines the usefulness of a Feelings Place. Some years it seemed to disappear into the wall from lack of use. Other classes used it every day. Once, the Feelings Place was in such high demand I had to establish some basic ground rules—you can only stay for three minutes and you have to clean up before leaving. If you find a student hiding out in the Feelings Place to avoid work, she is, of course, responsible for making up work.

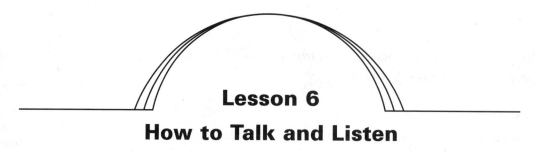

Lesson 6
How to Talk and Listen

Step 2 in the Problem-Solving Process

Purpose
▶ To help children express feelings in an assertive, nonthreatening way (I-message)
▶ To help children talk about what they need without making a demand (statement of need)
▶ To give children practice listening to I-messages and statements of need

Timing
Day 9

Materials
▶ How to Clear Clouds Away poster (see Appendix B)
▶ Clouds, various sizes (see Appendix A)
▶ Talk and Listen signs (see Appendix A)
▶ I-message, written on a sentence strip (described in this lesson)
▶ Need statement, written on a sentence strip (described in this lesson)

Procedure

1. Continue with the role-play from the previous lesson. Introduce and facilitate the talk and listen step.

Display the How to Clear Clouds Away poster with the last three steps covered. Tell students, "Remember yesterday when Katrina and Stephen had a problem with the puzzle? They were so upset they needed to cool off before they could start to *clear the clouds away*. Now that they are a little calmer, they are ready to find out what the problem is by talking and listening to each other. (Uncover step 2 on the poster.) Let's begin by figuring out what Stephen's part of the problem is. (Give Stephen the Talk sign.) Stephen, you talk first. Katrina, you listen. (Give her the Listen sign.) Then it will be your turn to talk. Now, Stephen, what happened?"

Listen as Stephen describes the problem from his perspective. Summarize his needs and feelings. For example, "So, you wanted to do the puzzle by yourself and you felt mad when Katrina kept trying to put in a piece. Is that right?" Before leaving Stephen's perspective, invite him to express his feelings and needs directly to Katrina using an I-message and need statement, described below. Offer help if necessary. For example, "Stephen, say to Katrina, I felt angry when you tried to do my puzzle. I want to do it by myself." Validate Stephen's assertive message and Katrina's listening. "Good job talking, Stephen. That was good listening, Katrina." Ask Katrina and Stephen to exchange their Talk and Listen signs.

Repeat the process with Katrina. Say, "Now, it is your turn to talk, Katrina. What happened?" Listen to her perspective and paraphrase her thoughts and feelings. For example, "So, you were trying to help Stephen by showing him where the piece goes. Is that right?" Ask Katrina to communicate her needs directly to Stephen. Help Katrina if necessary. For example, "Katrina, tell Stephen what you wanted. Say, 'I was trying to help.'"

Invite the class to validate Stephen and Katrina's skillful demonstration. "Let's clap and thank Stephen and Katrina for showing us how the talk and listen step works."

2. Review the speaking skills introduced above. Teach children how to make an I-message and a statement of need.

Say, "In step 2, when it is your turn to talk about your feelings, it works best to use an I-message." Show the sentence strip with the I-message formula:

I_____ when you_____.
    (feeling)   (specific behavior)

"When Stephen said, 'I felt angry when you tried to do my puzzle,' it was easy for Katrina to hear him because he did not blame her. He simply explained how he felt and what bothered him."

Introduce how to make a statement of need. Say, "In step 2, it is also helpful to talk about what you want or what is important to you." Show the sentence strip with the needs statement formula:

I want _____.

(what is important to you)

"When Stephen said, 'I want to do the puzzle by myself,' it helped Katrina understand why it bothered him when she tried to put in a piece."

"When it was Katrina's turn to talk, she also said what she wanted—'I was trying to help.' Then Stephen understood that she was not trying to make him mad or mess up his puzzle. She was just trying to be helpful."

Note: The I-message is more effective than a blaming "you" message because it tells the person how you (the speaker) are feeling without making the other person wrong. When you take responsibility for your feelings and what is bothering you, it is easier for the other person

3. Preview the last lesson.

Say, "Tomorrow we will learn the last two steps that finish *clearing* Stephen and Katrina's *clouds away.* Can anybody guess what needs to happen next?"

Ideas For Living the Lessons

I-message practice

Give children practice making I-messages. Describe a situation and ask, "Who can think of an I-message for this problem?" Here are some scenarios to get you started:

- ▶ You lend your friend a book and when it's returned, one of the pages is scribbled on.
- ▶ You're standing in line at the water fountain and someone pushes ahead of you.
- ▶ You are running in a race and you hear someone call you a slowpoke.
- ▶ A friend tells you she will play at recess, but when recess comes she runs off with other friends instead.
- ▶ Your friend keeps telling you what to do and doesn't listen to your ideas.

Model I-messages and need statements.

Children learn best by imitating your behavior. Use I-messages and make statements of need whenever you have feelings and desires to express. For example, "I get frustrated when you don't listen because then I have to repeat what I said." Or, "I need help cleaning the room."

to listen and think about making a change.

Sometimes you have other important information as well. What was the unmet need that accompanied the *cloudy* feeling and motivated your behavior? If you tell the person what you wanted, needed, or hoped would happen, he will better understand your perspective and how to solve the problem. Notice that the need statement works best when you talk from your perspective rather than when you make demands on the other person. For example, the statement "I need you to keep your hands off my puzzle" is not likely to be as effective as, "I want to do the puzzle by myself."

I-messages and need statements are sophisticated communication tools and difficult for children to use at first. Be on hand to correct them if they make a wrong turn and inadvertently *throw a cloud.* For example, if a student's I-statement comes out this way, "I feel like hitting you because you're so mean," suggest it be changed to, "I feel irritated when you touch my puzzle." Or, should a need statement sound like this, "I want you to stop hogging the puzzle," suggest the child try this, "I want a chance to do the puzzle, too."

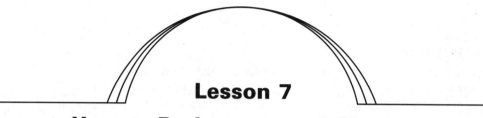

Lesson 7
How to Brainstorm and Choose

Steps 3 and 4 in the Problem-Solving Process

Purpose

▸ To increase children's skill in brainstorming solutions to social problems
▸ To increase children's skill in evaluating and choosing solutions that work for everyone involved

Timing

Day 10

Materials

▸ How to Clear Clouds Away poster (see Appendix B)
▸ Light bulb, the symbol for Brainstorming (see Appendix A)
▸ Idea Worksheet (see Appendix C)
▸ Two smiling suns, the symbol for Choosing (see Appendix A)
▸ Two large suns (see Appendix A)
▸ We Clear Clouds Away chart (described in Lesson 2)

Procedure

1. Review the role-play scenario used in Lessons 5 and 6. Introduce Step 3: Think of ways to solve the problem (brainstorm).

Display the How to Clear Clouds Away poster with the last two steps covered. Say, "Remember when Stephen and Katrina were pretending to have a problem with a puzzle? What were the first two steps they showed us that helped them begin to *clear the clouds away*?" (Cool off, and talk and listen.) "After they talked and listened to each other, they understood the problem better. They found out that Stephen wanted to do the puzzle by himself and Katrina wanted to help.

Now they're ready for the next step—think of ways to solve the problem." Uncover step 3 on the poster.

2. Invite children to brainstorm solutions to the problem.

Hold up the light bulb. Ask, "Who can remember what the light bulb means? (Brainstorm ideas. This step was first introduced in Lesson 4.) Let's find out how many different ways the puzzle problem could be solved. Who has an idea?"

As children offer ideas, write them on the chalkboard. Encourage the class to come up with as many ideas as possible. Keep restating the problem in terms of need and asking, "What else could they do so that Stephen has a chance to do the puzzle by himself and Katrina has a chance to help?"

Keep the pace quick and remember that all ideas are acceptable. If children comment about the ideas, remind them that feelings and thoughts about the ideas (their evaluations) belong in the next step.

3. Evaluate the ideas.

Uncover Step 4 on the poster. Say, "Now let's find out which ideas Stephen and Katrina will choose to solve the puzzle problem." Duplicate the format of the Idea Worksheet (Appendix C) on the board next to the list of ideas generated in the brainstorm. Beside each idea draw two blank faces. Write Stephen's name above the first column of faces and Katrina's above the second. Ask both children how they feel about the ideas listed and fill in the face with a smile, frown, or straight line, depending upon their response. A straight-line face means the idea is so-so—not a favorite, but one that might work.

4. Introduce and demonstrate Step 4: Choose the idea you both like. Find the idea or ideas with two smiling faces.

Hold up the Choose symbol (two smiling suns). Say, "It's easy to find the idea they both like because there are two smiling faces next to it." Read the win-win idea and ask Stephen and Katrina if that's the idea they both want to try. If there is more than one idea with double smiles, ask, "Of these two (or more) ideas, which one do you want to try first?" Children may also decide to combine a couple of their favorite ideas into their plan.

Note: Restating the problem in terms of need helps children go beyond the simplistic ideas they typically offer. If children say, "Be friends," accept that answer and encourage them to continue thinking. "What would friends do to solve the puzzle problem?" If children offer the solution, "Say sorry," accept the idea and ask, "What else would make the situation better for both?" (For more ideas about helping children make amends, see "'Sorry' Doesn't Always Fix It" on p. 126.)

Note: The brainstorming step is separated from the choosing step because judging inhibits the creative process and limits imagination. Discussion, criticism, and evaluation of ideas happen in Step 4.

"Sorry" Doesn't Always Fix It

When children are asked the question, "What can you do to solve the problem?" their answers often reflect what has worked for them. Many adults are satisfied if children apologize, so children oblige with a quick "sorry." This ends the matter and everyone returns to recess. Though a sincere expression of regret can soothe hurt feelings, a phony apology does little good. The offended child senses there is no real remorse, and because nothing is learned in the exchange, the problem often occurs again.

Instead of focusing on apologies, teachers can invite children to think of their own ways to make amends. "What can you do to fix the problem? How can you make it right?" A child who spills someone's basket of crayons might decide to pick up the crayons. A student who calls someone a name could say something nice or do a favor for the person whose feelings were hurt. Two children who push to be first at the water fountain can figure out how they can both get a drink without being hurtful. The time and effort required to remedy the situation discourages children from making the same mistake.

When children make restitution in their own way they not only benefit the person wronged, they heal themselves. Their effort to "make things right" restores their positive sense of self and moves them closer to becoming the kind of person they want to be (Gossen, 1998).

Note: If no idea receives two smiles, find the idea that is closest to a win-win solution (probably one that received a smile and a straight line) and ask how the idea might be changed so that it works better for both. Or, ask the two, "Do you have any new ideas?" For a more creative brainstorming session, involve the whole class.

5. Turn the idea into an action plan.

Ask Stephen and Katrina open-ended questions that make the solution concrete and specific. For example, if they decided that Stephen will do the puzzle by himself first and then Katrina will have a turn, ask, "What could Katrina do while Stephen is doing the puzzle. How will Katrina know when it is her turn?"

6. Act out the plan.

Say to Stephen and Katrina, "Now, act out the plan and see if it works to solve the problem." When they have acted out the final scene, ask Stephen and Katrina, "Did the idea work to *clear the clouds away*?"

Hand them both big suns and invite the class to clap and thank Stephen and Katrina for demonstrating how to *clear clouds away.*

7. Record the problem-solving example on the We Clear Clouds Away chart.

Write the role-player's names and their solution on the chart. For the example given, the teacher would record, "Stephen and Katrina took turns doing the puzzle."

8. Continue collecting examples of *clearing clouds away* and adding them to the We Clear Clouds Away chart.

The examples for the chart can be taken from more role-play scenarios you develop or from real social problems that occur in the class. Let students know that when *clouds are thrown,* you are available to guide them through the problem-solving process if they need help. The script in Appendix D will help you coach and support children to find their own solutions.

When helping youngsters find solutions to real problems, it often works best to ask them to evaluate the ideas as they are offered, rather than first generating a pool of ideas and evaluating them later. As the script suggests, after one child offers a solution, immediately ask the other, "Is that okay with you?" If the idea is rejected, continue seeking ideas and checking them out with the other child until they arrive at a solution they both like. If the two have trouble coming up with ideas, ask classmates for help.

Continue recording successes on the We Clear Clouds Away chart and reading the new entries daily. This reinforces the idea that "we are getting better and better at *clearing clouds away.*"

Ideas for Living the Lessons

Book of Solutions

Make a mental note of the problems your children experience, for example, not being able to find an eraser, being bored at recess, or getting a lunch they don't like. Periodically select a problem and invite the class to brainstorm solutions. For instance, "What can you do when a favorite friend isn't available to play?" As with any brainstorm, come up with many ideas without comments. Collect children's ideas

Note: Although young children can be guided to brainstorm many solutions to a hypothetical problem (as suggested earlier in this lesson and in Lesson 4), settling real-life conflicts is another matter. The emotions of the moment keep children very focused on their immediate needs and make it difficult for them to keep lots of ideas in mind. For this reason, the brainstorm rule about "no comments" may be relaxed when helping young children solve real problems.

on paper, write a statement of the problem at the top of the page and save the brainstorm for future use. Refer children to the list of solutions whenever the problem occurs.

Repeat the group brainstorming activity for other problems. Finally, bind the pages together and make a Book of Solutions for the class to refer to whenever these common problems arise.

Use children's books to reinforce problem solving.
During story time, point out concepts related to problem solving whenever they occur. Here are some basic understandings to note:

- Problems are a natural part of life and friendship.
- Problems can be handled in ways that lead to positive outcomes.
- Anger is natural and normal, as are other feelings. There is nothing wrong with any emotion.
- Some ways of expressing upsetting emotions make the problem worse. (The problem gets bigger.)
- Some ways of expressing upsetting emotions help solve the problem. (The problem gets smaller.)
- There is a relationship between our actions and what happens next; what we do affects us and others. (Cause-and-effect)
- There are many ways to solve a problem.
- We can often be creative enough to think of solutions that work for everyone.
- We are different from one another and we have many things in common.
- We see the world differently. There are different ways to see the same thing.
- Different points of view sometimes lead to misunderstandings. These misunderstandings can often be talked about and resolved.

Although many children's books involve social problems, the books listed on pp. 134–135 are especially well suited to exploring the problem-solving process. Here are some open-ended questions to help generate discussion with your students:

▶ What just happened? What is this problem about? (Define the problem.)

▶ How does ___ feel? How does ___ feel? How do you know? (Identify feelings. Empathize.)

▶ Why is ___ feeling *cloudy*? (Define the problem.)

▶ What do they each want? (Identify needs.)

▶ What do you think will happen next? (Predict outcomes.)

▶ Did that make the problem bigger or smaller? (Evaluate.)

▶ How could they solve the problem? (Brainstorm.)

▶ Did that *clear the clouds away*? Was that a fair solution? (Evaluate.)

▶ If ____ happened to you, what would you do? (Predict.)

Another way to use children's literature is to ask students to develop new endings to familiar stories or fairy tales. The new endings can then be illustrated, dramatized, or written. Imagine, for example, how the three billy goats might have resolved the situation with the troll if they tried to *clear the clouds away*. An excellent book on this topic is William Kriedler's *Teaching Conflict Resolution Through Children's Literature* (1994).

Encourage children to solve their problems without your help.
Although many youngsters will need your help to effectively solve their problems, with enough guided practice, some may become skillful enough to *clear clouds away* without your assistance. When skillful children report *clouds*, listen and validate their feelings as always, then escort them to the How To Clear Clouds Away poster. Point to the first step and ask if they need to cool off before proceeding. Pass out the Talk and Listen signs and invite the children to continue on their own.

Teacher Idea
Marie Crawford, a 3rd grade teacher at Fair Oaks School in Redwood City, California, discovered that students who were good at solving their problems independently were also skillful at facilitating the process for other students. After lunch she invited the *"cloud clearing"* helper of the day (a rotating job) to meet with students who

Note: Be sure to let children know that if communication breaks down, you are available to help. If, for example, when Mandy says to Charles, "I don't like it when you make fun of my freckles," Charles answers, "So!" then you need to intervene. Thank Mandy for doing a good job with the I-message, then talk with Charles privately. Find out what motivated Charles's hurtful response. If he was upset because Mandy laughed at his haircut, support Charles to express his upset feelings to Mandy in a more appropriate way, using an I-message.

Once they both have had a chance to talk and listen, continue with the process. The problem could be summarized this way: "So, it sounds like you both feel *cloudy* when people make fun of you. What would help you feel better now? The next time Charles has a haircut, what will you do differently, Mandy? If someone else makes fun of your hair, Charles, what can you do instead of *throwing* the *cloud* back?"

The scenario would play out differently if Charles was hurtful to Mandy for no apparent reason. For example, if Charles routinely *throws clouds* at others to get attention, Mandy's I-message would probably have little effect on his behavior. In this case, the teacher must intervene in a way that gives Charles the positive attention he needs and helps him change hurtful actions and become more caring in the future. Books in the Selected Resources section (p. 159) present respectful disciplinary strategies that support children to make such a change.

had problems, two at a time. The student helper then pointed to the How To Clear Clouds Away poster and moved the disputants through the steps by asking simple questions or giving instructions such as, "Are you cooled off enough?" "You talk first, you listen." "What ideas do you have to solve the problem?" "Which idea do you both like?" Marie also let the students know she was standing by to help if they got stuck.

Use puppets to reinforce problem-solving skills.

Find two "problem puppets" for your class. Puppets with arms work especially well because they can hold and throw things, grab, push, hit, shake hands, and hug. Introduce the problem puppets to your class and explain their purpose. Say, "I want you to meet Annie and Bunny. They're in 1st grade just like you. Usually they're good friends. But sometimes they have problems. Has that ever happened to you? The problem is that when Annie and Bunny get mad they often *throw clouds* at each other. They yell, call names, push, even hit sometimes. Do you think that makes the problem bigger or smaller? They *throw clouds* because they don't know what else to do. Will you teach Annie and Bunny how to *clear clouds away*?

Choose a typical or persistent problem for the puppets to act out. Because the puppets don't understand how to *clear clouds away*, they always do and say the wrong thing. Stop the play whenever the puppets *throw a cloud* and invite students to teach the puppets a better way. Refer students to the How to Clear Clouds poster as they move through the process. The script in Appendix D may help you coach the puppets to solve their problem.

Here is an example of how to use puppets to review and strengthen children's problem solving ability.

Teacher: (to puppets) Annie and Bunny, remember what happened on the monkey bars this morning?
Annie: Yeah, Bunny wouldn't give me a turn!
Bunny: Annie was mean! She pulled me off the monkey bars!
Annie: Then we really started *throwing clouds*.
Bunny: Yeah, and now Annie won't be my friend.

Teacher: Today the kids want to teach you how to *clear those clouds away* so you can be friends again. First, let's show the kids what happened.

(Annie and Bunny act out the problem.)

Teacher: (to children) Who can tell me what happened? (After children describe the problem, summarize it.) Yes, Bunny wanted to finish his turn on the monkey bars and Annie wanted a turn too. Did *throwing clouds* make the problem bigger or smaller? Let's teach Annie and Bunny how to *clear the clouds away*. (Display the How to Clear Clouds Away poster, Appendix B.)

1. Stop. Cool off.

Teacher: (to children) Who can tell Annie and Bunny what the first step is? (Cool off.) What does that mean? Who has an idea for Annie and Bunny about how they can cool off? (Ask children to brainstorm a number of cooling off strategies.)

Teacher: (to puppets) Which idea do you want to try?

(Annie and Bunny choose a cooling off idea and act it out.)

Teacher: (to puppets) Are you feeling a little better?

Puppets: Yes, a little.

2. Talk and listen.

Teacher: (to children) Okay, what's the second step? (Talk and listen.)

Teacher: (to puppets) Here, Annie, you talk first. (Give Annie the Talk sign.) And Bunny, you listen. (Give Bunny the Listen Sign, then address Annie.) Okay, Annie, what happened?

Annie: Bunny kept going back and forth on the monkey bars and he wouldn't let me have a turn.

Teacher: (to Annie) Okay, Annie, tell Bunny how you feel. Start with I.

Annie: I feel like punching you right in the face! (Look at Annie with a disappointed face.)

Teacher: (to children) Did that make the problem bigger or smaller? (Bigger) Who can think of better words for Annie to use?" (Children offer suggestions. Annie chooses an I-message and/or need statement and says it to Bunny.)

Annie: I felt *cloudy* when you took such a long turn on the monkey bars.

Teacher: Good, Annie. Also, tell Bunny what you want.

Annie: (to Bunny) I want a turn on the monkey bars.

Teacher: (to Bunny) What did you hear Annie say?"

Bunny: She wants a turn on the monkey bars.

Teacher: (to Bunny) Good listening, Bun!

(Switch the Talk and Listen Signs and repeat the second step with Bunny talking and Annie listening.)

Teacher: (to Bunny) Okay, Bunny, now it's your turn to talk. What happened?

Bunny: Annie pulled me off the monkey bars!

Teacher: (to Bunny) Okay, Bunny, tell Annie how you feel and what you want. Start with I.
Bunny: I felt *cloudy* when you pulled me off the monkey bars. I wanted to finish my turn.
Teacher: (to Annie) What did you hear Bunny say?"
Annie: He didn't like it when I pulled him off the monkey bars because he wanted to finish his turn.
Teacher: (to Annie) Good listening, Annie!

3. Think of ways to solve the problem.
Teacher: (to children) Okay, what's the third step? (Think of ways to solve the problem.) What can Annie and Bunny do so that Annie gets a turn on the bars and no one gets hurt? Let's count and see how many different ways the problem could be solved. Who has an idea? (Prompt students through the process of generating ideas. Keep track of the number and challenge them to come up with 10.)
Teacher: (to puppets) Did you hear all the ideas the children came up with?
Bunny: (obviously impressed) Yeah, and none of them were mean!

4. Choose the idea you both like.
Teacher: (to children) Okay, what's the last step? (Choose the idea you both like.)
Teacher: (to puppets) Annie and Bunny, which idea do you both like best?
(Annie and Bunny discuss their favorite ideas and finally arrive at one, or more, that they both like. If necessary, ask questions that help the puppets develop a specific action plan. For example, how long will each turn last?)

Teacher: (to puppets) Try out your plan and let's see how it works to *clear the clouds away.* (The puppets act out the idea they chose.)
Teacher: (to puppets) Are your *clouds cleared away?*
Puppets: Yes!
Teacher: (to children) Let's clap for Annie and Bunny!
Puppets: (to children) Thanks for teaching us how to *clear the clouds away!*

Lesson 7 Reading List

Children's Books with Problem-Solving Themes

Aliki (see Brandenberg)

Baker, B. (1969). *The pig war.* New York: HarperCollins.

Berenstain, S., & Berenstain, J. (1986). *The Berenstain bears and the trouble with friends.* New York: Random House.

Berenstain, S., & Berenstain, J. (1982). *The Berenstain bears get in a fight,* New York: Random House.

Blaine, M. (1975). *The terrible thing that happened at my house.* New York: Scholastic.

Brandenberg, A. (1993). *Communication.* New York: Greenwillow Books.

Clifton, L. (1974). *Three wishes.* New York: Dell Yearling.

Crary, E. (1982). *I can't wait.* Seattle, WA: Parenting Press.

Crary, E. (1982). *I want to play.* Seattle, WA: Parenting Press.

Crary, E. (1982). *I want it.* Seattle, WA: Parenting Press.

De Paola, T. (1980). *The knight and the dragon.* New York: G.P. Putnam's Sons.

De Paola, T. (1981). *The hunter and the animals.* New York: Holiday Books.

Erikson, R. (1974). *A toad for Tuesday.* New York: Lothrop, Lee and Shepard Co.

Gurney, N. & Gurney, E. (1965). *The king, the mice and the cheese.* New York: Random House.

Hoban, R. (1969). *Best friends for Frances.* New York: Harper and Row Publishers.

Hoban, R. (1970). *A bargain for Frances.* New York: Harper and Row Publishers.

Jones, R. (1991). *Matthew and Tilly.* New York: Dutton Children's Books.

Kellogg, S. (1973). *Island of the skog.* New York: Dial Books.

Lindgren, A. (1966). *The totem and the fox.* New York: Coward-McCann.

Lionni, L. (1963). *Swimmy.* New York: Alfred A. Knopf.

Lionni, L. (1985). *It's mine!* New York: Alfred A. Knopf.

Lionni, L. *(1988). Six crows.* New York: Alfred A. Knopf.

Polacco, P. (1992). *Chicken Sunday.* New York: Philomel Books.

Roth, C. (1988). *Whose mess is this?* New York: Western Publishing Co.

Seuss, Dr. (1984). *The butter battle.* New York: Random House.

Udry, J. (1961). *Let's be enemies.* New York: HarperCollins.

Wildsmith, B. (1971). *The owl and the woodpecker.* Oxford: Oxford University Press.

Yashima, T. (1955). *Crow boy.* New York: Viking Press.

Zolotow, C. (1969). *The hating book.* New York: HarperCollins.

Activity 1
Illustrate the Story

Purpose
▶ To review *The Rainbow Kids Story*
▶ To make a class book with drawings of favorite scenes
▶ To help children identify with the characters by putting themselves "into the picture"

Timing
Day 3, after finishing the story; this is an optional activity.

Materials
▶ White drawing paper (11" X 18"), approximately one sheet per child
▶ Crayons or markers
▶ A cover page
▶ Hole punch and yarn

Procedure

1. Prepare blank pages for the illustrations.
Punch holes on one side of each piece of paper (prepare at least one piece of paper for each student).

2. Introduce the art activity.

Distribute the paper to the students, with appropriate directions about the side of the paper you want students to draw on. Tell them you'd like them to illustrate *The Rainbow Kids Story* by drawing a favorite scene. Ask children to draw themselves in their pictures and to include suns, clouds, and rainbows as appropriate for the scene they select. Students may choose any scene, not just the ones in which they appear in the story. Also, allow them to change their roles by telling them "When I put your name in the story, I didn't know which part you'd want. If you wish you had a different part, draw yourself in a role you like better." This gives children a chance to "become" the character they most strongly identify with.

3. Call out the scenes and ask for volunteers to illustrate them. Here are suggestions.

Cover illustration: Suggest a picture of Rainbow Valley or ask students to make suggestions for the cover.

Part I: the picnic; the marble spill; the surprise party; kids 15 and 16 leave the valley in search of Zeke; kids 15 and 16 camp outside the hidden cave; Zeke peeks outside the cave and sees rainbows in the valley

Part II: Zeke grabs the apple from kid 17; kid 18 comforts kid 17, who is now *cloudy*; Zeke pushes at the water fountain; Zeke grabs toys at the playground and *throws clouds*; Zeke kicks the toys in his cave; the kids *throw clouds* at each other and end up under thick clouds; kids 15 and 16 fall asleep in front of Zeke's cave; Zeke drags kid 16 and his light to his dark corner; kids 15 and 16 discover Zeke in the morning; kid 15 runs down the hill to get the other kids

Part III: the hide-and-seek game; the *storm* between Julie and Dennis; kid 15 helps Julie and Dennis *clear clouds away*; the kids follow kid 15 to Zeke's cave; the kids light up the cave (Zeke has a sun, too); the line of rainbows marching home

Distribute paper and art supplies. Children may work alone or with partners. As students are choosing their favorite scene to illustrate, do not expect every scene in the story to be illustrated. Several children may choose the same scene. Other scenes may not be chosen at all.

4. Write about each picture.

Circulate among the children as they work and take dictation or help them write sentences or stories describing the scenes they chose.

5. Assemble the book.

Arrange the pages to correspond with the story and tie them together with yarn. Write the title on the cover page and give a byline (insert your room number or the name of your class, if you have one). Share the finished product with the class and make the book available in the class library.

Fun with Rainbows

When I first developed the *Rainbow Kids Program*, northern California was in the fifth year of a drought. Not only had my 1st graders never seen a rainbow in the sky, but they also had not experienced much rain. To make rainbows come alive we created our own with prisms and by turning on the sprinkler one sunny morning. We discovered that rainbows naturally occur in other places as well—near waterfalls, on the edge of a sunlit aquarium, and on soap bubbles. Some animals have a rainbow pattern of coloring. Iridescent colors can be found on some insect shells, on the scales of some fish, and on the throat feathers of hummingbirds and pigeons. Incidentally, the word iridescence is from the Greek word *iris*, which means "rainbow." In Greek mythology, Iris was the goddess who traveled down the rainbow to bring messages to the people on earth. For more information, check out *The Rainbow and You* (Krupp, 2000), a delightful and informative children's book that explores the science and mythology of rainbows.

Teacher Ideas

When Peggy Garland's 2nd grade class in Millbrae, California, was preparing to illustrate their *Rainbow Kids* story, they realized they weren't sure about the order of the colors in the rainbow. This led them to the library, where they researched the topic and discovered a handy way to remember—ROY G BIV (red, orange, yellow, green, blue, indigo, and violet; red is on the outside of the arc and violet is on the inside.) After that, the children meticulously made their rainbow colors in the proper sequence.

Julie Johnson, a Kindergarten teacher in Gainesville, Florida, found that rainbow crayons inspired her children to put rainbows into their artwork. Each 2½-inch crayon includes red, orange, yellow, green, and blue. The crayons, which are called "Striper Crayons," can be ordered from Discount School Supply, 800-627-2829. Julie's children also made colorful oil pastel drawings of rainbow kids on "Neopolitan Construction Paper" (which looks like rainbows on paper), available from Nasco Arts and Crafts (800-558-9595).

Sandy Sale, a teacher in Atherton, California, integrates math into the *Rainbow Kids Program* by graphing her students' favorite rainbow colors. She also dyes macaroni in seven colors and has her Kindergarteners make necklaces in the rainbow pattern. To dye macaroni, fill a plastic bag halfway with macaroni and add a couple capfuls of rubbing alcohol and a few dashes of food coloring or liquid watercolor. Close the bag and shake. Spread the macaroni on paper to dry. Rainbow necklaces can also be made with brightly colored, circular-shaped breakfast cereals.

Carla Gomann, another Atherton, California, teacher, makes home-made play dough in rainbow colors for her students.

Nori Yost of Ponderosa School in South San Francisco, California, made rainbow rice for her Kindergarteners. Yost dyed the rice by adding 1/4 teaspoon rubbing alcohol and a couple drops of food color to a cup of raw rice and stirring it quickly. She dried the rice in the sun (spread out on paper). Her children used the six colors of rice for a variety of art projects. She even made a "rice" table for them.

Donna Habeeb, a parent volunteer at Gill School in Redwood City, California, helped the class make tie-dye rainbow shirts. To get a rainbow effect, the shirts were gathered into several "sunburst" patterns, tied with rubber bands and dyed with primary colors.

Sue Sartor, a Kindergarten teacher in Atherton, California, designed a rainbow cloud by drawing a cloud shape on a large piece of white construction paper and stapling seven tissue or construction paper strips in rainbow colors on the lower edge of the cloud. To make the cloud "puffy," she cut a second cloud in the same shape, and stapled it to the first cloud. Before closing the "pocket," she stuffed it with newspaper.

Activity 1 Reading List

Children's Books About Rainbows

Freeman, D. (1966). *A rainbow of my own.* New York: Viking Press.

Kalan, R. (1978). *Rain.* New York: Greenwillow Books.

Kirkpatrick, R. K. (1985). *Rainbow colors.* Milwaukee: Raintree Childrens Books.

Krupp, E. C. (2000). *The rainbow and you.* New York: HarperCollins.

Kuskin, K. (1957). *James and the rain.* New York: HarperCollins.

Shannon, D. (2000). *The rain came down.* New York: Blue Sky Press.

Tabor, N. M. B. (1997). *We are a rainbow.* Watertown, MA: Charlesbridge Publishing.

Zolotow, C. (1952). *The storm book.* New York: HarperCollins.

Activity 2
Empathy Game

Purpose
- To introduce empathy as a desirable skill
- To give children practice being sensitive to the feelings of others
- To let children experience the empathy of others

Timing
Any time after Lesson 1; this activity is optional.

Materials
- Two chairs
- Two suns and clouds
- Empathy stories (examples included)

Procedure

1. Introduce the game.

Talk about dress-up play and the fun of pretending to be someone else. Then say, "Today we're going to pretend to be someone else, but instead of trying on clothes, we're going to try on another person's feelings and see if we can guess if the person is feeling *sunny* or *cloudy*." Hold up a sun and a cloud.

Discuss with children why it is desirable to be able to tune into another's feelings. Point out that people who can guess the feelings of others, or empathize, are good at *spreading sunshine* because they can figure out what makes someone feel *sunny*. Also, if you know how others feel, you are less likely to *throw clouds* because you can predict whether an action is hurtful or not. It is also helpful to understand other's feelings when looking for ways to *clear clouds away*.

Note: Surprisingly, children love this simple game and often ask to repeat it. They easily identify with the scenarios and feel whatever emotion the story elicits because their names are used. Although only two children actively play the game at one time, the classmates who watch the play also empathize with the players each time a story is read.

The Empathy Game is especially effective with children who don't naturally consider other's feelings. With a little effort, you can give those students the experience they most need. For example, a child who repeatedly bosses others around would benefit from sitting in either seat and listening to a story about a bossy person. Be sure to change the story's circumstances enough so that children don't recognize the real story or involved child. Use the sample stories or make up your own with particular students in mind.

After children have played the game, remind them about trying on feelings whenever it is appropriate. For example, when Kristin grabs all the markers in the basket, you could say, "Kristin, I notice you have all the markers at your table. Try on the feelings of the children sitting near you. What you could do so that everyone feels *sunny?*"

2. Set up and play.

Ask children to gather in a circle, either in chairs or on the floor. Put two chairs in the center of the circle, one behind the other. Invite two children to sit in the chairs. Give them both a sun and a cloud to hold in their laps. Tell a story (samples below) about the child in the front seat. At the end of the story, ask the child in the first seat to hold up a sun or a cloud, depending on how she feels. The symbol should be held so that the child sitting behind can't see it. Then ask the child sitting behind to "try on" or empathize with the first child by guessing her feelings. The second child does this by holding up a sun or cloud. A correct guess ends the round, and two more children take the seats for another story.

For example, Erin sits in the front chair and Jasper is behind her. The teacher reads this story. "Erin just finished reading a book by herself. She is very excited and tells one of her friends. Someone overhears her and says, 'Oh, that's nothing. I finished that book in Kindergarten!' How does Erin feel?" Erin holds up a cloud. The teacher asks Jasper, "Try on Erin's feelings. Does she feel *sunny* or *cloudy*?" Jasper makes a guess and holds up a cloud. The teacher asks the class, "Was Jasper right?" Everyone claps for Jasper and another round begins.

Sample Stories

▶ During sharing time you leave the circle to get something special out of your cubby. When you get back, someone is sitting in your place. You ask the person, "Could you please move? I was sitting there." The other person replies, "Find your own place! I'm sitting here!" How do you feel?

▶ You are making a watercolor painting. Someone says, "My water is cleaner than yours." How do you feel?

▶ You are the line leader. Every time you line up that day, the same person tries to cut ahead of you. How do you feel?

▶ You just finished a game of kickball and your team lost. Someone from the other team comes over to you and says, "Good game!" and pats you on the back. How do you feel?

▶ You are walking in line. The person behind you is walking so close he steps on your heel. How do you feel?

▶ You have just finished drawing a picture of a horse. Someone sitting near you says, "That's neat! Will you show me how you made it?" How do you feel?

▶ You are sitting on the floor watching a movie. The person ahead of you is on her knees and it's hard for you to see. You say to her, "I can't see." "SO!" the person replies. How do you feel?

▶ You can't find your eraser. Someone sitting next to you says, "Here, you can borrow mine." How do you feel?

▶ The teacher asks a question and calls on you. You think real hard and give your best answer. It turns out the answer isn't right. A couple of kids laugh at your mistake. How do you feel?

▶ You are walking to the water fountain. Someone bumps into you. "Oh, I'm sorry. It was an accident. Are you all right?" How do you feel?

▶ You are tearing out a page in your workbook. You accidentally rip the paper. Someone hands you a piece of tape. How do you feel?

▶ The teacher puts a basket of new markers on your table. One of the kids sitting near you grabs six of them. How do you feel?

▶ Someone brings a special toy to share. You ask him if you can see it. "Sure! You can play with it at recess." How do you feel?

▶ You and your friend both want the same silent reading book. Your friend says, "Go ahead—you read it first. When you're done, will you please give it to me?" How do you feel?

▶ You are playing with a new friend. You hear someone nearby say (taunting tone),

"Look, _____ is playing with
(name)

a _____." How do you feel?
(girl/boy).

Appendix A
Symbols

Use these patterns for the weather symbols to bring the rainbow kids' feelings to life. Although you can use nearly any medium, I recommend felt or construction paper. Paper symbols show up best if the edges are outlined with black marker. Here's what you'll need.

Two rainbows (same size); plus one tiny rainbow for Zeke
The rainbow can be drawn on white construction paper. Use markers or oil pastels to color the rainbow. The order of the colors are (from outside to inside) red, orange, yellow, green, blue, indigo, and violet (ROY G BIV).

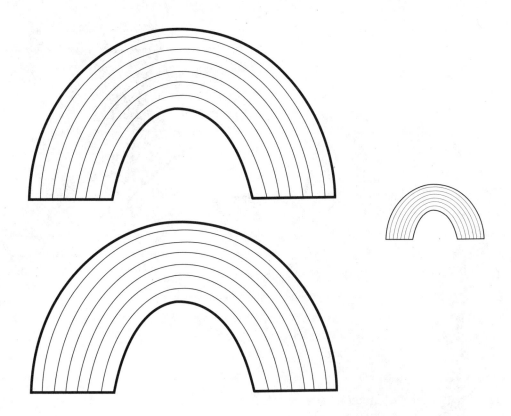

Three suns of different sizes; plus a tiny sun sun for Zeke

The suns can be made from yellow construction paper or flannel.

Three clouds of different sizes

The clouds can be made from gray construction paper or flannel. Use yellow construction paper or flannel to make the lightning bolts for the large cloud.

Talk and Listen Signs

Copy the pictures of the mouth and ear and mount them on heavy paper or cardboard. Attach each to a small stick (e.g., popsicle stick, straw, or unsharpened pencil) so that children can hold them up in Step 2, as they take turns talking and listening.

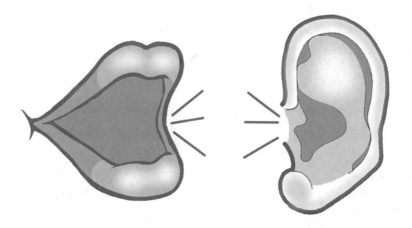

Clearing Clouds Away Symbol

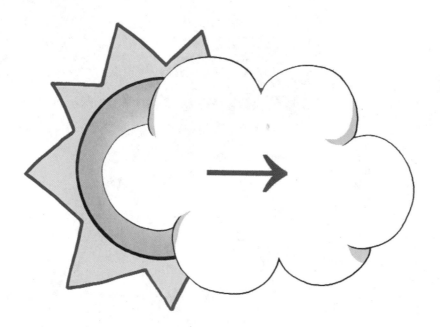

Cool Off symbol

Brainstorm symbol

Choose symbol

Appendix B
How to Clear Clouds Away

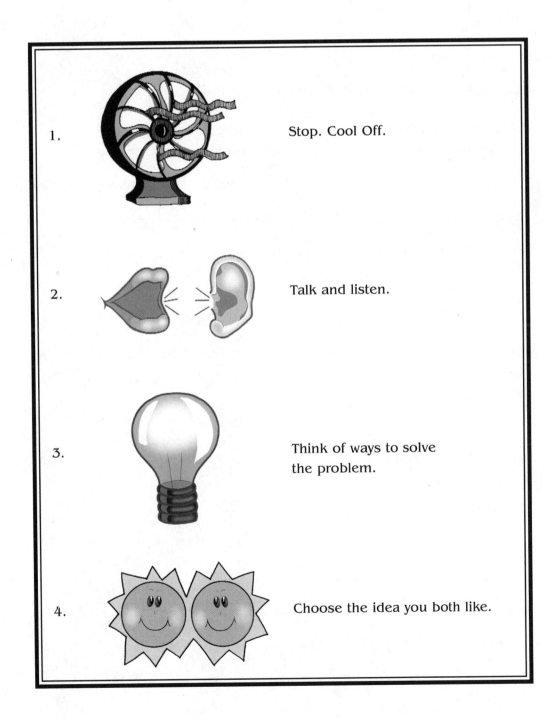

1. Stop. Cool Off.

2. Talk and listen.

3. Think of ways to solve the problem.

4. Choose the idea you both like.

Appendix C
Idea Worksheet

What can we do so that _____ (Child #1) gets what he needs and
_____ (Child #2) gets what she needs?

Here are ideas about how
we can solve the problem:

Here's how we feel
about each idea:

(child #1)   (child #2)

☐ _____   ◯   ◯

☐ _____   ◯   ◯

☐ _____   ◯   ◯

☐ _____   ◯   ◯

☐ _____   ◯   ◯

☐ _____   ◯   ◯

☐ _____   ◯   ◯

Check the box in front of the idea or ideas we both like.

Appendix D

How to Help Children Clear Clouds Away

When children come to you with problems, guide them through the 4-step process using this facilitator's script.

1. Stop. Cool off.

Get on children's level. Speak calmly.

"It looks like you have a problem. Would you like help *clearing clouds away*?"

"May I have the _____ (object they are fighting over) please?"

"Let's take a deep breath and cool off for a moment."

2. Talk and listen.

"You'll both have a turn to talk. _____ (child 1) talks first. Then it will be _____ (child 2)'s turn."

To _____ (child 1): "What happened?" Paraphrase his response.

"Tell _____ (child 2) how you feel (and what you want). Start with I."

("I feel _____ when you _____.")

To _____ (child 2): "What happened?" Paraphrase her response.

"Tell _____ (child 1) how you feel (and what you want). Start with I."

("I want _____.")

Summarize: "It sounds like _____ (child 1) wants _____ and _____ (child 2) wants _____."

3. Think of ways to solve the problem.

To both children: "How can you solve the problem so you'll both be happy (*sunny*)?"

One child offers a solution.

Ask the other child, "Is that okay with you?"

Continue eliciting ideas and checking them out with the other child.

4. Choose the idea you both like.

Continue with Step 3 until children arrive at a solution they both like. Ask questions that help children make a plan. For example:

"How will you share it?"

"How will you decide who goes first?"

"How long will each turn last?"

Offer the children your congratulations. "You did a good job *clearing clouds away!*"

Appendix E
Sunny Songs

Here are some popular songs that have a *sunny* theme. Teach them to students to reinforce the concepts presented in the *Rainbow Kids Program*.

There's a Little Wheel A-Turnin'   —American Folk Song

There's a little wheel a-turnin' in my heart,
There's a little wheel a-turnin' in my heart,
In my heart, in my heart
There's a little wheel a-turnin' in my heart.

There's a little song a-singin' in my heart,
There's a little song a-singin' in my heart,
In my heart, in my heart,
There's a little song a-singin' in my heart.

There's a little sun a-shinin' in my heart,
There's a little sun a-shinin' in my heart,
In my heart, in my heart,
There's a little sun a-shinin' in my heart.*

  *Verse 3 added by Barbara Porro

This Little Light   —Traditional
(chorus)
This little light of mine, I'm gonna let it shine.
This little light of mine, I'm gonna let it shine.
This little light of mine, I'm gonna let it shine,
let it shine, let it shine, let it shine.

You Can Make the Sun Shine   —Traditional

You can make the sun shine any old time,
Even when the skies are gray.
You can make the sun shine any old time,
Even when the skies are gray.
You can make the sun shine.
You can make the sun shine any old time,
Even when the skies are gray.

Magic Penny

—Words and music by Malvina Reynolds, (©1955 MCA-Northern Music Corp. (ASCAP). Used by permission.

(chorus)
Love is something if you give it away
Give it away, give it away
Love is something if you give it away
You end up having more

It's just like a magic penny, hold it tight and you won't have many
Lend it, spend it and you'll have so many,
They'll roll all over the floor, for (chorus)

So let's go dancing till the break of day,
And if there's a piper, we can pay,
For love is something if you give it away,
You end up having more.

Money's dandy and we like to use it
But love is better if you don't refuse it
It's a treasure and you'll never lose it
Unless you lock up your door.

It's just like the new spring flowers,
If you cut them off, they'll only last a few hours,

Give them sun and rain and lots of care,
And you'll have blossoms everywhere, 'cuz (chorus)

It's just like a paper kite,
You hold it tight and it can't take flight
Let it go and it will soar so high
It'll fly right up to the sky, 'cuz (chorus)

Look for more *sunny* songs in the following songbook and recordings.

Bos, B., & Leeman, M. (1987). May there always be sunshine and rainbow round me (Songs). *Hand in Hand* (Audiotape). Turn the Page Press.

Disney. (2001). Zip-A-Dee-Doo-Dah (Song). *Disney's greatest*, vol. 1. (Audio CD). Uni/Disney.

Hamilton, A. (1989). Sing a rainbow (Song). *Sing a rainbow big book*. (Songbook). Salem, OR: Nellie Edge Resources.

Jenkins, E. (1989). I know the colors in the rainbow (Song). Koch, F. *Did you feed the cows? Fred Koch presents the songs of Ella Jenkins*. (Audio CD). ASIN.

Raffi. (1998). One light, one sun. (Song). *One light, one sun* (Audiotape). Uni/Rounder.

Appendix F
Sample Parent Letter

Dear Parents,

Next week we will begin working with a new social skills program called the *Rainbow Kids*. The program is based upon a story about us! (Each student's name appears in the story.) I'd like to acquaint you with the program so that if you begin hearing "Rainbow Kid" language at home, you will know what your child is talking about.

The goal of the program is to help children become aware of their feelings and actions and how their behavior affects others. The kids in the story have a special quality—whatever they are feeling inside appears as weather outside them. So, for example, when the kids feel happy, their suns shine big and bright. Whenever they say or do something kind for someone else (the kids call this *spreading sunshine*), their suns grow bigger than before. This teaches children that when they extend their positive feelings to others, everyone benefits. It often rains in the valley where the kids live and when it does, they enjoy dancing and playing in the rain. As their light shines through the raindrops, rainbows appear around them. That's why they're called the rainbow kids.

Later in the story the kids are hurtful toward one another and clouds appear in front of their suns. Each time the kids retaliate with more hurtful gestures, the clouds grow bigger. This points out that when children *throw clouds* (are hurtful), upset feelings increase and the problem gets bigger for everyone. At the end of the story the kids figure out how to *clear the clouds away* by resolving their problems respectfully. Here children learn that when feelings get hurt, it is possible to talk about the problem and find solutions that work for everyone.

After hearing the story, we will practice *spreading sunshine* (openly caring about others) and *clearing clouds away* (solving problems). The 4-step problem-solving process is simple: (1) Stop. Cool off; (2) Talk and listen; (3) Think of ways to solve the problem; and (4) Choose the idea you both like.

If you have any questions about the program or if you want to hear more, don't hesitate to call me.

Sincerely,

(Your name)

Selected Resources for Elementary Teachers

Classroom Management and Discipline

Albert, L. (1989). *Cooperative discipline: Classroom management that promotes self-esteem*. Circle Pines, MN: American Guidance Service.

Charney, R. S. (1992). *Teaching children to care: Management in the responsive classroom*. Greenfield, MA: Northeast Foundation for Children.

Faber, A., & Mazlish, E. (1995). *How to talk so kids will learn at home and at school*. New York: Rawson Associates.

Gootman, M. (2001). *The caring teacher's guide to discipline*. Thousand Oaks, CA: Corwin Press.

Gordon, T. (1970). *Teacher effectiveness training*. New York: Peter Werden.

Gordon, T. (1989). *Discipline that works*. New York: Penguin Books.

Gossen, D. C. (1998). *Restitution: Restructuring school discipline*. Chapel Hill, NC: New View Publications.

Kohn, A. (1993). *Punished by rewards: The problem with gold stars, incentive plans, A's, praise, and other bribes*. Boston: Houghton Mifflin.

Kohn, A. (1996). *Beyond discipline: From compliance to community*. Alexandria, VA: Association for Supervision and Curriculum Development.

Nelson, J. (1987). *Positive discipline*. New York: Ballantine Books.

Nelson, J., & Glenn, H. S. (1991). *Time out: Abuses and effective uses*. Fair Oaks, CA: Sunrise Books.

Social and Emotional Skills Curriculums and Materials

Child Development Project. (1996). *Ways we want our classroom to be: Class meetings that build commitment to kindness and learning*. Oakland, CA: Developmental Studies Center.

Cihak, M., & Heron, B. (1980). *Games children should play: Sequential lessons for teaching communication skills in grades K-6*. Glenview, IL: Scott, Foresman.

Crary, E. (1984). *Children's problem solving series (Ages 3-8)*. Seattle, WA: Parenting Press.

Dalton, J., & Watson, M. (1997). *Among friends: Classrooms where caring and learning prevail*. Oakland, CA: Developmental Studies Center.

Drew, N. (1987). *Learning the skills of peacemaking*. Rolling Hills Estates, CA: Jalmar Press.

Elias, M., Zins, J., Weissberg, R., Frey, K., Greenberg, M., Haynes, N., Kessler, R., Schwab-Stone, M., & Shriver, T. (1997). *Promoting social and emotional learning: Guidelines for educators.* Alexandria, VA: Association for Supervision and Curriculum Development.

Gibbs, J. (1987). *Tribes: A process for social development and cooperative learning.* Santa Rosa, CA: Center Source Publications.

Kriedler, W. (1990). *Elementary perspectives 1: Teaching concepts of peace and conflict.* Cambridge, MA: Educators for Social Responsibility.

Kriedler, W. (1994). *Teaching conflict resolution through children's literature.* New York: Scholastic Professional Books.

Kriedler, W. (1998). *Early childhood adventures in peacemaking.* Cambridge, MA: Educators for Social Responsibility.

Kriete, R. (1999). *The morning meeting book.* Greenfield, MA: Northeast Foundation for Children.

Levin, D. E. (1994). *Teaching young children in violent times: Building a peaceable classroom.* Cambridge, MA: Educators for Social Responsibility.

Pirtle, S. (1998). *Discovery time for cooperation and conflict resolution.* Nyack, NY: Children's Creative Response to Conflict.

Porro, B. (1996). *Talk it out: Conflict resolution in the elementary classroom.* Alexandria, VA: Association for Supervision and Curriculum Development.

Prutzman, P., Stern, L., Burger, M. L., & Bodenhamer, G. (1988). *The friendly classroom for a small planet.* Nyack, NY: Children's Creative Response to Conflict.

Sadalla, G., Holmberg, M., & Halligan, J. (1987). *Conflict resolution: An elementary school curriculum.* San Francisco, CA: Community Board Program.

Sapon-Shevin, M. (1999). *Because we can change the world.* Needham Heights, MA: Allyn & Bacon.

Schiller, P., & Bryant, T. (1998). *The values book: Teaching 16 basic values to young children.* Beltsville, MD: Gryphon House.

Shure, M. (1992). *I can problem solve: An interpersonal cognitive problem-solving program.* Champaign, IL: Research Press.

Stone-McCown, K., Jensen, A., Freedman, J., & Rideout, M. (1998). *Self science: The emotional intelligence curriculum.* San Mateo, CA: Six Seconds.

Strachota, B. (1996) *On their side: Helping children take charge of their learning.* Greenfield, MA: Northeast Foundation for Children.

Wood, C. (1994). *Yardsticks: Children in the classroom ages 4-14.* Greenfield, MA: Northeast Foundation for Children.

Wood, C. (1999). *Time to teach, time to learn: Changing the pace of school.* Greenfield, MA: Northeast Foundation for Children.

General Reading About Emotional Intelligence

Goleman, D. (1995). *Emotional Intelligence: Why it matters more than IQ.* New York: Bantam Press.

Salovey, P., & Sluyter, D. (Eds.). (1997). *Emotional development and emotional intelligence: Educational implications.* New York: BasicBooks/HarperCollins.

Parent Education

Beekman, S., & Holmes, J. (1993). *Battles, hassles, tantrums and tears: Coping with conflict and creating a peaceful home.* New York: Hearst Books.

Cline, F., & Fay, J. (1990). *Parenting with love and logic.* Colorado Springs, CO: Navpress

Coloroso, B. (1994). *Kids are worth it: Giving your child the gift in inner discipline.* New York: Morrow and Co.

Crary, E. (1984). *Kids can cooperate.* Seattle, WA: Parenting Press.

Elias, M., Tobias, S., & Friedlander, B. (1999). *Emotionally intelligent parenting.* New York: Harmony Books.

Faber, A., & Mazlish, E. (1980). *How to talk so kids will listen and listen so kids will talk.* New York: Avon Books.

Faber, A., & Mazlish, E. (1987). *Siblings without rivalry.* New York: Avon Books.

Gottman, J. (1997). *Raising an emotionally intelligent child.* New York: Simon & Schuster.

Seligman, M. (1995). *The optimistic child.* New York: HarperCollins.

Shure, M. B. (2000). *Raising a thinking child workbook: Teaching young children how to resolve everyday conflicts and get along with others.* Champaign, IL: Research Press.

References

Elias, M., Zins, J., Weissberg, R., Frey, K., Greenberg, M., Haynes, N., Kessler, R., Schwab-Stone, M., & Shriver, T. (1997). *Promoting social and emotional learning: Guidelines for educators.* Alexandria, VA: Association for Supervision and Curriculum Development.

Fabes, R. A., Fultz, J., Eisenberg, N., May-Plumlee, T., & Christopher, F. S. (1989). Effects of rewards on children's prosocial motivation: A socialization study. *Developmental Psychology 25*(4): 509–515.

Goleman, D. (1995). *Emotional intelligence: Why it matters more than IQ.* New York: Bantam Press.

Greenberg, M. T., Kusche, C. A., Cook, E. T., & Quamma, J. P. (1995). Promoting emotional competence in school-aged children: The effects of the PATHS curriculum, *Development and Psychopathology 7*(1): 117–136.

Gossen, D. C. (1998). Restitution: Restructuring school discipline. Chapel Hill, NC: New View Publications.

Grusec, J. E. (1991). Socializing concerns for others in the home. *Developmental Psychology 27*(2): 338–342.

Hawkins, J. D., Catalano, R. F. (Eds.). (1992). *Communities that care.* San Francisco: Jossey Bass.

Jensen, A. (1999, June). Emotional intelligence certification course (Lecture). At Six Seconds Professional Development Institute, Menlo Park, CA.

Kohn, A. (1990). *The brighter side of human nature: Altruism and empathy in everyday life.* New York: Basic.

Korb, P., Gorrell, J., & Van De Riet, V. (1989). *Gestalt therapy: Practice and theory.* New York: Pergamon Press.

Porro, B. (1996). *Talk it out: Conflict resolution in the elementary classroom.* Alexandria, VA: Association for Supervision and Curriculum Development.

Seligman, M. (1995). *The optimistic child.* New York: HarperCollins.

Shure, M. B., & Spivack, G. (1982). Interpersonal problem solving in young children: A cognitive approach to prevention. *American Journal of Community Psychology, 10*(3): 341–356.

Stone-McCowen, K., Jensen, A., Freedman, J., & Rideout, M. (1998). *Self science: The emotional intelligence curriculum.* San Mateo, CA: Six Seconds.

Wolfe, P. (1999, March 3–5). Translating brain research into instructional practices (Workshop). At Professional Development Institute, ASCD Conference, San Francisco, CA.

Index

About the Author

Barbara Porro is a dynamic and entertaining staff developer. Since 1989, she has conducted hundreds of conflict resolution and social skills workshops for teachers, students, and parents nationwide. Her knowledge and insights about classroom life are based on 14 years of elementary teaching experience. Barbara holds two master's degrees in education (University of Florida and Stanford University) and is also the author of *Talk it Out: Conflict Resolution in the Elementary Classroom* (ASCD, 1996). She is now Director of the Caring School Community Program with Developmental Studies Center, a nonprofit educational organization in Oakland, California.

Porro may be reached at 298 King St., Redwood City, CA 94062 USA. E-mail: Bporro@aol.com. Additional information is available at www.Barbaraporro.com. For information about teacher workshops, call 800-684-2729.

Rainbow Kids **Response Form**

Now that you have read about my experience, tell me about yours. I welcome your comments, suggestions, ideas, and questions. I will pass them on to other teachers, with credit to you. Please send your comments by mail or e-mail.

1. What worked well for you and your students?

2. What didn't work?

3. What changes would you suggest?

4. Do you have any new ideas or materials to share?

5. What are your questions?

If you offer new ideas, please tell me about you so that I can give you credit.

Name_____

City and State_____

Grade level _____

If you choose, you may include your school and full address in your response.

Thank you,
Barbara Porro
298 King St.
Redwood City, CA 94062 USA
Bporro@aol.com

Related ASCD Resources:
Conflict Resolution, Character Education

ASCD stock numbers are noted in parentheses.

Audiotapes

Character Development Through Cooperative Strategies by Spencer Kagan (#200178)

Creating a Community with Character by David Archibald (#200071)

Educating for Character in a New Century by Rushworth Kidder (#200207)

How Not to Teach Values: A Critical Look at Character Education by Alfie Kohn (#296112)

Networks

Visit the ASCD web site and search for "networks" for information about professional educators who formed groups around topics like "Character Education," "Conflict Resolution," and "Early Childhood Education."

Print Products

As Tough As Necessary: Countering Violence, Aggression, and Hostility in Our Schools (#197017)

Character Education (*Educational Leadership*, v. 51, n. 3; #611–93175)

Connecting Character to Conduct: Helping Students Do the Right Things by Rita Stein, Roberta Richin, Richard Banyon, Francine Banyon, and Marc Stein (#100209)

Connecting with Students by Allen N. Mendler (#101236)

Discipline with Dignity, rev. ed., by Richard L. Curwin and Allen N. Mendler (#199235)

Every Child Learning: Safe and Supportive Schools by Learning First Alliance (#301279)

Reducing School Violence Through Conflict Resolution by David W. Johnson and Roger T. Johnson (#195198)

Talk It Out: Conflict Resolution in the Elementary Classroom by Barbara Porro (#196018)

The Soul of Education: Helping Students Find Connection, Compassion, and Character at School by Rachael Kessler (#100045)

Videotapes

Character Education: Restoring Respect and Responsibility in Our Schools by National Professional Resources, Inc. (#396286)

For additional resources, visit us on the World Wide Web (http://www.ascd.org), send an e-mail message to member@ascd.org, call the ASCD Service Center (800-933-ASCD or 703-578-9600, then press 2), send a fax to 703-575-5400, or write to Information Services, ASCD, 1703 N. Beauregard St., Alexandria, VA 22311-1714 USA.

About ASCD

Founded in 1943, the Association for Supervision and Curriculum Development is a nonpartisan, nonprofit education association, with international headquarters in Alexandria, Virginia. ASCD's mission statement: *ASCD, a diverse, international community of educators, forging covenants in teaching and learning for the success of all learners.*

Membership in ASCD includes a subscription to the award-winning journal *Educational Leadership*; two newsletters, *Education Update* and *Curriculum Update*; and other products and services. ASCD sponsors affiliate organizations in many states and international locations; participates in collaborations and networks; holds conferences, institutes, and training programs; produces publications in a variety of media; sponsors recognition and awards programs; and provides research information on education issues.

ASCD provides many services to educators—prekindergarten through grade 12—as well as to others in the education community, including parents, school board members, administrators, and university professors and students. For further information, contact ASCD via telephone: 800-933-2723 or 703-578-9600; fax: 703-575-5400; or e-mail: member@ascd.org. Or write to ASCD, Information Services, 1703 N. Beauregard St., Alexandria, VA 22311-1714 USA. You can find ASCD on the World Wide Web at http://www.ascd.org.

ASCD's Executive Director and Chief Executive Officer is Gene R. Carter.

2002-03 Executive Council Members

Peyton Williams Jr. *(President)*, Raymond J. McNulty *(President-Elect)*, Kay A. Musgrove *(Immediate Past President)*, Pat Ashcraft, Martha Bruckner, Mary Ellen Freeley, Richard L. Hanzelka, Douglas E. Harris, Mildred Huey, Susan Kerns, Robert Nicely Jr., James Tayler, Andrew Tolbert, Sandra K. Wegner, Jill Dorler Wilson

Belief Statements

Fundamental to ASCD is our concern for people, both individually and collectively.

- We believe that the individual has intrinsic worth.
- We believe that all people have the ability and the need to learn.
- We believe that all children have a right to safety, love, and learning.
- We believe that a high-quality, public system of education open to all is imperative for society to flourish.
- We believe that diversity strengthens society and should be honored and protected.
- We believe that broad, informed participation committed to a common good is critical to democracy.
- We believe that humanity prospers when people work together.

ASCD also recognizes the potential and power of a healthy organization.

- We believe that healthy organizations purposefully provide for self-renewal.
- We believe that the culture of an organization is a major factor shaping individual attitudes and behaviors.
- We believe that shared values and common goals shape and change the culture of healthy organizations.